SEASIDE Adventure

A programme to develop fine and gross motor skills in nursery settings

LDA

Acknowledgements

I should like to thank the whole, wonderful team who have been involved in producing this programme, starting with Yvette Ostermeyer (former senior advisory teacher for physical impairment) and the medical professionals: Helen Burrows (paediatric occupational therapist), Sara Christie (former paediatric physiotherapist) and Sara Orr (paediatric physiotherapist). This team wrote the original Development of Early Motor Skills (DEMS) programme, now known as *The Jungle Journey*. The collaboration between health and education has resulted in the production of very useful materials to aid development of gross and fine motor skills in young children. The same team penned the *Seaside Adventure* programme and then trusted us to get on with the project trials and make any necessary little changes. I hope we have lived up to their expectations.

I should like to thank Carol Palin (advanced skills teacher for PE), who has been involved in all DEMS training sessions for at least five years and who has contributed to the supplementary materials. Carol's expertise in and knowledge of early PE skills were instrumental to the success of the project.

Thank you to Becky Tyler, and particularly to Janet Davies and Janet Lee, early years district SENCos, who have also contributed to the materials and to the success of the pilot project.

My thanks also go to Helen Gibson (former early years advisory teacher) and the team of early years advisory practitioners – Fiona Baddeley, Nicola Buss, Marie Woodward and particularly Lesley Wilkie – for their contributions to the programme and also for their hard work in producing the very useful additional planning guidance for settings.

Thank you to the nursery settings who agreed to take part, and to the Community and Learning Partnerships Stafford 4 and South Staffs 3, 4 and 5, who enabled us to carry out the final phase of the pilot project.

Finally, a special thank you to Sandra Swift (head of Special Educational Needs Support Service) for her continued sponsorship and belief in the value of the programme.

Rachel Knight Editor
(DEMS Coordinator, SENSS, Staffordshire LA)

Permission to photocopy

The right of Staffordshire County Council to be identified as the author of this work has been asserted by them in accordance with sections 77 and 78 of the Copyright, Designs and Patents Act 1988.

The *Seaside Adventure* CD provides electronic files of the sessions and additional support materials.

Seaside Adventure
MT11713
ISBN-13: 978 1 85503 494 5

© Staffordshire County Council
Illustrations by Baz Rowell and Rebecca Barnes
All rights reserved
First published 2011

Printed in the UK for LDA
LDA, Findel Education, Hyde Buildings, Ashton Road, Hyde, Cheshire, SK14 4SH

Contents

Foreword

Following on from the success of *The Jungle Journey*, which focused on the Reception or Primary 1 stage, *Seaside Adventure* provides an exciting new, easy-to-use and well-designed programme from the same team. *Seaside Adventure* focuses on the Early Years stage and shows how to improve motor skills in those who may need some additional exposure and experience.

Early identification of delay or difficulty and provision of support and guidance can make a profound difference to children's future functioning. There is evidence that without early intervention children may enter primary school with less confidence in their approach to play and less ability to participate with others. This may have a secondary negative effect on their self-esteem.

Motor skills are an essential part of the repertoire every child requires for functioning. Without good co-ordination children cannot learn to write, to use tools such as scissors and rulers or to play, and cannot participate in sports and self-care. All of these skills are vital to maximise every child's potential and also for each child to remain physically well, not only in the short term but also in the longer term.

Much of the focus in the past few years has been on gaining literacy and numeracy skills. With a greater emphasis in the Early Years curriculum on exploration and play, perhaps now motor skills will take their rightful place as a core skill to recognise for all, especially at this crucial time of a child's development.

The activities in *Seaside Adventure* have been devised by practitioners with lengthy experience of working with children who have motor difficulties, and this is evident from their design. This book is a welcome contribution in assisting Early Years practitioners in both identifying those who may need some additional help, and providing the guidance and ideas to do so.

Professor Amanda Kirby
The Dyscovery Centre
University of Wales, Newport

Dedication

This book is dedicated to the memory of Ruth Rowley (Head of SENSS, Staffordshire 2003–2009), without whose support and belief this programme would not have been developed.

1 About the programme

Introduction to the programme

Seaside Adventure is designed to be carried out with those children in nursery settings who are in their final year before starting school. It is suitable for those with a wide range of physical abilities. The programme has two major objectives:

1. It has been written to help improve the motor competence of a large number of children who, for a variety of reasons, have not achieved appropriate developmental norms in terms of their fine and/or gross motor skills. It is widely recognised that movement competence may determine the extent to which a child is able to perform effectively within the school environment, and indeed it is a prerequisite for maximum access to the school curriculum. The acquisition of motor skills influences intellectual, social and emotional development.

2. Through observation of the children during the programme and the screening process included in *Seaside Adventure*, early years practitioners will find it easier to identify those children who are having particular difficulties in physical development, possibly as a result of an underlying problem rather than lack of early opportunity and experience. Concerns about persisting difficulties should be shared with parents and ideally with the child's first teacher at a transition meeting. Passing screening results on to school will help with careful monitoring of progress. Further intervention may be required such as the use of the *Jungle Journey* programme.

Seaside Adventure is written with a child-friendly approach, which will enable motor potential to be maximised and therefore improve learning outcomes. However, the children will benefit in particular from taking part in activities which focus on the following areas:

- proximal stability – this encompasses shoulder girdle, pelvic girdle, abdominal and back extensor activity; good trunk stability is a requirement for balance and is a prerequisite for fine motor control;
- hand–eye co-ordination;
- proprioceptive feedback;
- motor planning;
- auditory and visual sequencing;
- symmetrical, bilateral and reciprocal integration of movement.

> **Note:** If a child with a known medical condition (e.g. cerebral palsy) is present in the setting, it is vital that advice from the child's physiotherapist or occupational therapist is sought before beginning the programme. The child may have difficulties with the programme, and it may conflict with their current treatment plan.

The programme has been written bearing in mind the health, safety and welfare of the children taking part. However, if at any time practitioners feel that any of these are being compromised by the activities, it is expected that they will make appropriate modifications to the programme.

The suggested format of the programme is as follows:

1. Pre-programme screening of all children taking part in the programme

2. Preparation period (up to 4 weeks)

3. Delivery of the programme over a 9-week period
   Gross motor: 1 x 20-minute session per week
   Fine motor: 3 x 10–15-minute sessions per week

4. Post-programme screening.

The pre- and post-assessments make it easy for early years practitioners to evaluate the success of their teaching in addition to measuring the progress of the children.

Background to the programme

Seaside Adventure was written following the success of a similar programme, The Jungle Journey, which was designed to develop early motor skills in children of Reception class age. The concept for such a programme had originally come about as a consequence of a very heavy caseload for the advisory teacher for physical impairment, Yvette Ostermeyer, and lengthy waiting lists for medical professionals including paediatric physiotherapists and occupational therapists. The referrals made were for an increasing number of children who were displaying dyspraxic tendencies. When the children were eventually seen, most of their motor difficulties were found to be due not to a specific difficulty but rather to lack of early experience. When allowed further opportunities to practise their fine and gross motor skills, many children caught up to age-appropriate levels. At the same time, research with nursery-age children had been carried out in the north of England by Madeleine Portwood, an educational psychologist. Her findings were alarming:

> *Having completed a recent study to examine the motor-competency of more than four hundred 3-year-old pupils in nurseries in County Durham, I was not surprised to discover that just over half of those assessed achieved at the level of skill expected for children of that age. One cannot assume that almost 50 per cent of 3-year-olds should be labelled as having a 'developmental coordination disorder' but what is the explanation and what is the effect on future learning outcomes?* (Portwood 2004)

Movement skills are very important, and it is widely accepted that movement is the basis for all learning.

> *Movement is a child's first language – it is the first medium of expansion of the physical and emotional conditions of an individual. Self-control begins with the control of movement.* (Goddard Blythe 2000)

> *The change in our society over the past 40 to 50 years – particularly in respect of family lifestyle – appears to have had a detrimental effect on our children in many ways, including the development of language and of early motor skills.* (Goddard Blythe 2004, Palmer 2006 – both summarised)

> *Since the young brain is better equipped to adapt, the sooner intervention can be put into place for children with movement difficulties, the better. It is also important to avoid the negative impact poor motor skills can have on self-esteem as the child gets older.* (Macintyre and McVitty 2004 – summarised)

Rather than simply trying to cope with the increasing number of referrals, Yvette Ostermeyer from education and her colleagues from health worked collaboratively on a programme designed to accelerate the development of motor skills in children who had simply lacked early opportunity. The intention was for children with real movement difficulties to be seen and helped sooner. The programme was designed to be carried out with the whole class. This takes responsibility away from class teachers, who may not be confident in identifying those children who need extra intervention. This distinguishes the programme from other well-researched motor skills programmes. The programme was tried and tested with active and control schools with very positive results, culminating in some children making huge progress in fine and/or gross motor skills. The programme was then rolled out across Staffordshire, and since then more than 65 per cent of schools in the county with Reception age pupils have attended training.

Early years practitioners in nursery settings, who heard about the success of the *Jungle Journey* programme, have frequently asked when a similar programme would be written for younger children. *Seaside Adventure* is that programme. It has been tried and tested with active and control settings and results were again very positive. There are now plans to introduce this programme into nursery settings across Staffordshire.

Links to the Early Years Foundation Stage curriculum

❙❙ Every child deserves the best possible start in life and support to fulfil their potential. A child's experience in the early years has a major impact on their future life chances. A secure, safe and happy childhood is important in its own right, and it provides the foundation for children to make the most of their abilities and talents as they grow up. ❙❙

Statutory Framework for the Early Years Foundation Stage (2008), DCSF

The *Seaside Adventure* programme helps children to move towards many of the early learning goals, as follows.

Personal, Social and Emotional Development (PSED)

By the end of the Early Years Foundation Stage (EYFS), children should:

- continue to be interested, excited and motivated to learn;
- be confident to try new activities, initiate ideas and speak in a familiar group;
- maintain attention, concentrate, and sit quietly when appropriate;
- respond to significant experiences, showing a range of feelings when appropriate;
- form good relationships with adults and peers;
- work as part of a group or class, taking turns and sharing fairly, understanding that there need to be agreed values and codes of behaviour for groups of people, including adults and children, to work together harmoniously;
- dress and undress independently and manage their own personal hygiene;
- select and use activities and resources independently.

Communication, Language and Literacy (CLL)

By the end of the EYFS, children should:

- interact with others, negotiating plans and activities and taking turns in conversation;
- enjoy listening to and using spoken and written language, and readily turn to it in their play and learning;
- sustain attentive listening, responding to what they have heard with relevant comments, questions or actions;
- listen with enjoyment, and respond to stories, songs and other music, rhymes and poems and make up their own stories, songs, rhymes and poems;
- extend their vocabulary, exploring the meanings and sounds of new words;
- use language to imagine and re-create roles and experiences;
- use talk to organise, sequence and clarify thinking, ideas, feelings and events.

Problem Solving, Reasoning and Numeracy (PSRN)

By the end of the EYFS, children should:

- say and use number names in order in familiar contexts;
- count reliably up to ten everyday objects;
- in practical activities and discussion, begin to use the vocabulary involved in adding and subtracting;
- use language such as 'more' or 'less' to compare two numbers;
- find one more or one less than a number from 1 to 10;
- use language such as 'greater', 'smaller', 'heavier' or 'lighter' to compare quantities;
- talk about, recognise and re-create simple patterns;
- use language such as 'circle' or 'bigger' to describe the shape and size of solid and flat shapes;
- use everyday words to describe position.

Knowledge and Understanding of the World (KUW)

By the end of the EYFS, children should:

- investigate objects and materials by using all of their senses as appropriate;
- find out about, and identify, some features of living things, objects and events they observe;
- select the tools and techniques they need to shape, assemble and join materials they are using;
- find out about past and present events in their own lives, and in those of their families and other people they know;
- observe, find out about and identify features in the place they live and the natural world.

Physical Development (PD)

By the end of the EYFS, children should:

- move with confidence, imagination and in safety;
- move with control and co-ordination;
- travel around, under, over and through balancing and climbing equipment;
- show awareness of space, of themselves and of others;
- recognise the importance of keeping healthy, and those things which contribute to this;
- recognise the changes that happen to their bodies when they are active;
- use a range of small and large equipment;
- handle tools, objects, construction and malleable materials safely and with increasing control.

Creative Development (CD)

By the end of the EYFS, children should:

- respond in a variety of ways to what they see, hear, smell, touch and feel;
- express and communicate their ideas, thoughts and feelings by using a widening range of materials, suitable tools, imaginative and role-play, movement, designing and making, and a variety of songs and musical instruments;
- recognise and explore how sounds may be changed, sing simple songs from memory, recognise repeated sounds and sound patterns and match movements to music;
- use their imagination in art and design, music, dance, imaginative and role-play and stories.

Planning guidance and preparation

Seaside Adventure is designed to be implemented as part of a main theme for all the children in the setting, and this way has proved to be most successful. Although the sessions are written as discrete activities, there is a wealth of additional material to be found on the accompanying CD. This provides some effective suggestions for continuous provision during the nine weeks over which the programme runs. Use of these fun, additional activities will ensure that the children gain full advantage of the programme, while complying with advice for best practice as recommended in the *Practice Guidance for the Early Years Foundation Stage* (May 2008).

Also on the CD there are suggestions for preparing the children for the programme. These consist of adult-led activities and continuous provision that may be used for up to four weeks of preparation. It was felt that this was a necessary addition as the programme requires much use of imagination and role-play. If the children are unfamiliar with concepts that they are asked to imagine or have never visited the seaside, they may find it difficult without such groundwork. Much of the new vocabulary is introduced at this stage, in order for the children to be able to participate fully when the programme commences. These additional activities were compiled by a team of early years advisory practitioners led by an early years advisory teacher, all well versed in the recommendations of the EYFS curriculum. Nursery settings now have the flexibility to allow their younger children to benefit from the continuous provision activities, even if they do not take part in the specially designed group sessions for those of pre-school age.

2 Screening

Guidelines for screening

Introduction

The screening tool is an integral part of *Seaside Adventure*, and has proved to be very effective in measuring the amount of progress made by a child in terms of their motor development. It is designed to be carried out immediately preceding the nine-week programme and again immediately following its completion, and a comparison of the two scores is made for each child.

The activities that make up the screening tool are based on norms for motor development for 3-year-old children. (Guidelines for fine and gross motor skills are included in this book.) There are six gross motor and six fine motor activities. It is expected that those who are not much over 3 years of age when first screened will not perform as well as those a few months older, and this should be taken into consideration.

It is hoped that by taking part in *Seaside Adventure* children will have opportunities for developing movement competency which have not previously been available to them, and that their skills will develop accordingly. The screening tool is a useful method of recording their progress.

There may be a few children who, as a direct result of the screening, are identified as not having made sufficient progress. It is important that this information is shared with parents or carers. To comply with good practice, a transition meeting should be arranged with the child's new school to discuss concerns and possible courses of action. This may include taking part in the *Jungle Journey* programme during the Reception year.

How to carry out the screening process

It is vital that each child is observed individually during the screening so that an accurate assessment can be made of their ability in each and every activity. Children's skills may vary from one activity to another, to a quite surprising extent in some cases. The organisation of the screening will depend on the resources available, both in terms of space and people, and it is important to realise that it is quite time consuming. However, the information that will be gathered is well worth the time spent obtaining it.

The same person should carry out the assessment both preceding and following the completion of the programme, to ensure consistency of scoring.

The assessment criteria should be read carefully before commencement of the screening to make sure that the activities are carried out correctly.

You will need to photocopy the activity sheets required for Assessment Tasks 7 and 9 before starting screening.

General observations relating to the activities

Assessment Tasks 1–4 (gross motor) – best carried out by the children barefoot; this will make it easier to observe more accurately what they are doing.

Assessment Tasks 1–6 (gross motor) and 12 (fine motor) – it is advisable to demonstrate these to the children first, so that they know exactly what is required of them.

Assessment Tasks 7–10 – only the instructions explaining what has to be done should be given. It is very important that children are not allowed to compare what they are doing with each other or copy others' ideas.

Additional observations should be made while the children are carrying out Assessment Tasks 7–10 (fine motor). These will not contribute to the scoring, but will provide useful information to be used when drawing up Foundation Stage Profiles on the development of writing. These will include noting the following:

- ✪ Whether the child swaps hands when holding the pencil, or uses only the dominant hand.
- ✪ Pencil grasp (tripod grasp).
- ✪ How the child is sitting at the table.
- ✪ Whether the non-writing/drawing hand is used to keep the paper still.

Scoring

A record sheet (Photocopiable 1, p. 19) is supplied for the screening. You will need to photocopy this before you begin screening. A notebook will be useful for any additional observations you wish to make; use a separate page for each child.

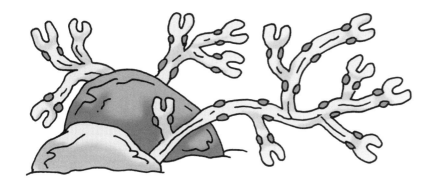

Gross motor assessment criteria

Assessment Task 1: One leg balance

Equipment needed: stopwatch/watch may be used

DESCRIPTION	CRITERIA/OBSERVATIONS	PERFORMANCE/SCORE
Balance on 1 leg – test both legs in turn. Child should be in a clear space away from walls and furniture. On 1 leg, arms freely at the sides, lifted leg bent backwards at the knee so that the foot is positioned behind the standing leg.	Bent leg does not have to stay at 90° angle but must be kept off the floor and away from supporting leg. Swaying is allowed and arms may move from sides. Hopping is not allowed – the supporting foot should remain in the same place on the floor. Note that accurate timing is important – use a stopwatch if possible or count '1 lobster pot, 2 lobster pot, 3 lobster pot', etc.	**3** = 5 seconds as in criteria – with either right or left leg **2** = momentary balance (2 seconds) on either leg – this should be controlled (i.e. not keeping 1 foot off the ground while falling over) **1** = makes attempt but unable to balance on 1 leg **0** = does not attempt to stand on 1 leg

Assessment Task 2: Jump with feet together

Equipment needed: 2 round plastic spots (diameter 20 cm)

DESCRIPTION	CRITERIA/OBSERVATIONS	PERFORMANCE/SCORE
Jump from 1 plastic spot to land on a second plastic spot. Distance between plastic spots should be 1 spot width (20 cm).	From a stationary position, with the feet together, jump from 1 spot to the other. Land with both feet meeting the floor simultaneously, feet together or apart. Demonstrate first.	**3** = take off / landing feet together on the second spot – up to 3 attempts **2** = lands with 1 foot after the other on the second spot **1** = maintains feet together position while jumping, but landing on or near the first spot **0** = unable to lift both feet off the ground simultaneously

Assessment Task 3: Hopping

Equipment needed: none

DESCRIPTION	CRITERIA/OBSERVATIONS	PERFORMANCE/SCORE
Demonstrate 4+ hops with right and then left foot.	Hops may be on the spot or travelling forwards but should follow on immediately from the one before. The raised foot should not touch the ground between hops. The adult should count the number of hops.	**3** = 2–4 hops achieved with right and left foot **2** = single hop on right **and** left foot **1** = attempts the beginnings of a hop but foot does not leave the ground **0** = no attempt at hopping

Assessment Task 4: Stand, walk, run

Equipment needed: none

DESCRIPTION	CRITERIA/OBSERVATIONS	PERFORMANCE/SCORE
Standing, walking and running with heels raised.	The child should attempt to stand, then walk, then run, all on the balls of the feet. Heels should remain clear of the floor.	**3** = able to stand, walk and run on the balls of the feet with heels raised: arms should remain relaxed, moving loosely at sides **2** = able to stand and walk as above, but unable to run **1** = able to go up and stand on the balls of the feet if shown **0** = unable to stand on balls of feet, heels raised

Assessment Task 5: Throw/catch

Equipment needed: 1 beanbag, 1 large ball, 1 small ball

DESCRIPTION	CRITERIA/OBSERVATIONS	PERFORMANCE/SCORE
A – child should catch 1–4 out of 10 beanbags thrown from a distance of 2 m; catch should be away from the body, not against the chest. **B** – if child is unable to catch a beanbag, catch large ball instead on or between extended arms and hands (i.e. hands away from the body, not against the chest). **C** – if child unable to catch, use smaller ball and observe throwing instead.	The beanbag should be caught cleanly in the hands and not just gathered to the body (hands may be brought in to the body after the catch). The beanbag or large ball should be thrown so that it reaches the child's hands at about chest height. If the throw arrives above the shoulders, below the waist or out of reach, it should not be counted, and a further attempt should be allowed. It is acceptable for the child to have up to 5 practice catches before counting begins.	**3** = 1–4 catches achieved, caught cleanly away from the body **2** = catches large ball 1–4 times on or between extended hands **1** = able to throw a small ball overhand in forward direction without losing balance and able to throw a small ball underarm between waist + chest height **0** = unable to throw ball as above

Assessment Task 6: Walk up/down stairs/steps

Equipment needed: stairs/steps

DESCRIPTION	CRITERIA/OBSERVATIONS	PERFORMANCE/SCORE
Observe the child walking / assist the child to walk up and down several stairs/steps.		**3** = able to walk up and down stairs in an adult fashion (i.e. places 1 foot on to each step in turn) **2** = able to walk up and down stairs as above, needs to hold on to wall/rail **1** = walks up and down stairs placing 2 feet on to each step **0** = has great difficulty in walking up and down stairs

Fine motor assessment criteria

Assessment Task 7: Tracing along a line

Equipment needed: photocopied sheet of the pencil track (Photocopiable 2, p. 20), pencil

DESCRIPTION	CRITERIA/OBSERVATIONS	PERFORMANCE/SCORE
Place the printed sheet with fish/boat track horizontally on the table. Place a pencil on the sheet with the point facing towards the child. Ask the child to pick up the pencil and draw along the waves, from the fish to the boat, trying to stay between the lines.	The child draws within the guidelines. Note whether they swap hands with the pencil. Note pencil grasp (tripod grasp?). How is the child sitting at the table? Do they hold the paper still?	**3** = deviates from the line no more than twice **2** = deviates from the line 3–4 times **1** = deviates from the line more than 4 times **0** = does not follow direction of the line

Assessment Task 8: Screwing/unscrewing a lid

Equipment needed: small container with screw-top lid

DESCRIPTION	CRITERIA/OBSERVATIONS	PERFORMANCE/SCORE
The child is presented with a bottle with a 2.5 cm screw-top lid. Ask the child to undo the lid. A small object may be placed in the bottle, which they get out. They may then be asked to put the object back in the bottle and screw the lid back on.	The child may be shown how to do this or given verbal prompts as a trial. Then they should try again without assistance. Observe whether the child understands how to get the lid off. Does the child first need a demonstration or verbal prompts?	**3** = child is able to screw and unscrew the lid **2** = child is able to perform 1 action (can usually unscrew the lid but not screw it) **1** = child makes an attempt and does some of the right actions but is unsuccessful in doing either **0** = child has no idea how to unscrew or screw the lid

Assessment Task 9: Copying shapes

Equipment needed: photocopied sheet with pre-drawn shapes (Photocopiables 3a and 3b, pp. 21, 22), dry sand / shaving foam / thick paint in a tray

DESCRIPTION	CRITERIA/OBSERVATIONS	PERFORMANCE/SCORE
A paper with pre-drawn shapes is placed on a table for child to refer to. Ask the child to copy the shapes in the sand / shaving foam / finger paint or other appropriate medium using their finger. Shapes are not intended to be copied on to paper. The child should not be shown how to draw the shapes.	The child copies these shapes: Observe whether the child can isolate the index finger. Does the child need a demonstration before being able to draw the shape?	**3** = child copies 4–5 shapes correctly **2** = child copies 3 shapes correctly **1** = child copies 1–2 shapes correctly **0** = no shapes are copied correctly

Assessment Task 10: Threading beads – timed

Equipment needed: stopwatch or 30-second timer, 8 round wooden beads (25 mm) in a container, a lace for threading

DESCRIPTION	CRITERIA/OBSERVATIONS	PERFORMANCE/SCORE
Place a box of round wooden beads on the table in front of the child. Ask the child to thread the beads on to the lace as fast as they can. Demonstrate how to thread a bead on to the lace and let it drop to the bottom. Ask the child to stand up and hold the string in their drawing (dominant) hand. It should still have 1 bead on to weigh it down. Let the child thread 2 beads as a practice. Then time the child threading the beads for 30 seconds. If the child drops a bead tell them not to pick it up. If they drop the string, they start again.	Note whether the child uses a pincer grasp to hold the lace. Does the child keep swapping hands to hold the lace?	**3** = child threads 3 or more beads **2** = child threads 2 beads **1** = child threads 1 bead **0** = child is unable to thread any beads

Assessment Task 11: Dressing

Equipment needed: none

DESCRIPTION	CRITERIA/OBSERVATIONS	PERFORMANCE/SCORE
Observe the child when putting on a coat, shoes and socks and taking them off.	Observe whether the child attempts to do some fastenings e.g. Velcro shoes, pulling up zips if started for them and attempting buttons. Be aware that some socks may be very tight and hinder the child. Observe putting on socks, not tights. Tight trainers may need loosening around the laces to let the child slip the shoe on/off.	**3** = child is able to put on / remove coat, shoes and socks, receiving assistance only with fastenings **2** = child is able to take off and put on 2 items (usually shoes and socks but not coat); help with fastenings allowed **1** = child can remove clothing but not put it on **0** = child requires full assistance

Assessment Task 12: Finger opposition

Equipment needed: none

DESCRIPTION	CRITERIA/OBSERVATIONS	PERFORMANCE/SCORE
Ask the child to make a circle first with the thumb and index finger on 1 hand, then the thumb and each finger in turn. Repeat with the other hand.	The child is able to oppose their thumb to each finger on both hands. Note the accuracy of the tips of the fingers/thumb meeting. This can be observed when doing hand rhymes / nursery rhymes.	**3** = child is able to oppose thumb to all fingers on both hands **2** = child is able to make a fist and isolate the thumb and index finger; thumb and finger can then be put together to form a circle **1** = child can isolate finger and/or thumb on 1 hand **0** = child is unable to isolate or oppose any finger or thumb

Screening tool record sheet

Assessment task			GROSS MOTOR							FINE MOTOR							
			One leg balance	Jump	Hopping	Stand, walk, run	Throw/catch	Walk up/down stairs	Total	Tracing along a line	Screw/unscrew lid	Copying shapes	Threading beads	Dressing	Finger opposition	Total	
Name	Date	Age	M/F	1	2	3	4	5	6		7	8	9	10	11	12	

Fish and boat track

Name ....

Date ....

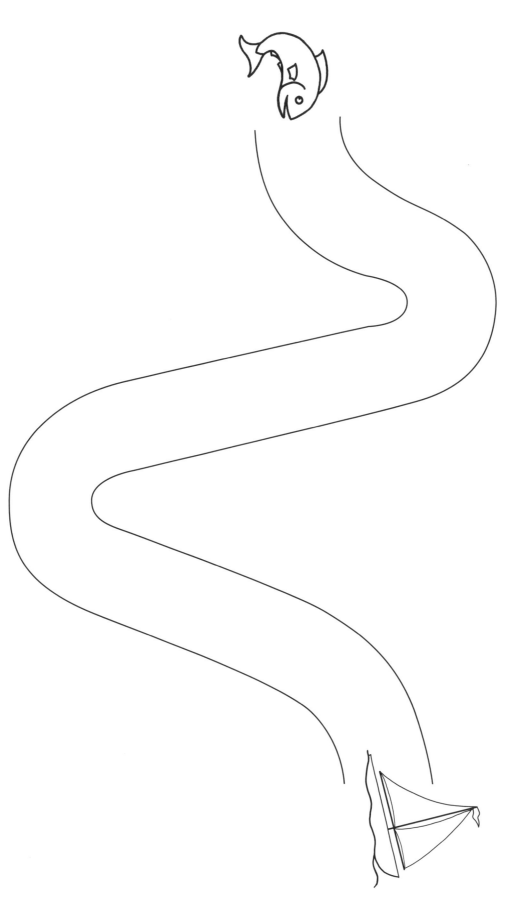

Copy the shapes

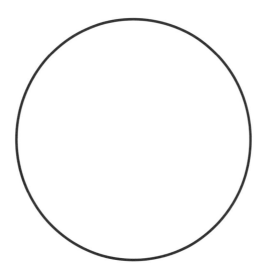

Copy the shapes

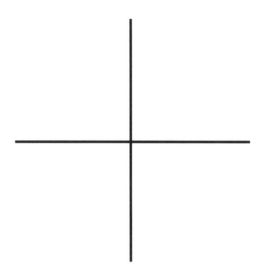

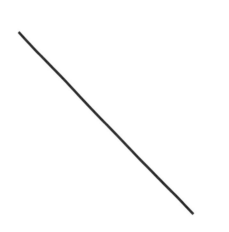

3 The programme

Gross motor sessions

Weeks 1–9 25

Fine motor sessions

Weeks 1–9 50

Gross motor sessions

Week 1: Getting ready

Aims

- To experience changes of level
- To travel in different directions
- To develop trunk stability

Equipment needed

- **Warm-up:** None
- **Strength:** Small towel per child, 1 large bag
- **Skill:** Bucket and spade per child; CD track 20: Seaside atmosphere

WARM-UP

NARRATION	ACTION
It's time to wake up. Have you remembered what day it is today? Open your eyes. Turn your head slowly to see if anyone else is awake.	The children lying on backs as if in bed, open eyes and turn heads slowly, looking around.
It's time to get up and get ready to go to the seaside! Roll over on to your side to see if everyone is awake now. Roll on to the other side just to make sure.	Roll over on to 1 side and then the other. They pretend to throw their quilts back.
Come on, out of bed now, or we shall miss the bus! Let's crawl slowly down to the ends of our beds.	The children crawl on hands and knees, as if crawling down to the end of the bed.
We still feel very sleepy! Let's stretch up high to wake ourselves up. Let's shake ourselves all over.	They stretch up as high as they can, then relax and shake all over. Repeat actions.
Have you remembered that we are going to the seaside today? The sun is shining and we are going to have a wonderful time! Let's jump and shout 'Hooray!'	The children jump up in the air, taking off from 2 feet and stretching arms up, and shout 'Hooray!'

STRENGTH

Gross motor week 1

NARRATION	ACTION
We need to get our buckets and spades to take with us. We had better look for them. Let's stretch up tall and look on top of the wardrobe.	The children stretch up as high as they can with heels raised from floor and arms straight up above the head, fingers outstretched.
They're not there! Perhaps they are under the bed. We'll have to crawl right underneath to look.	Commando crawl along the floor, lying on tummies and using bent arms to pull body along. Legs remain outstretched and still.
I think they are right at the back by the wall. Can you reach them?	Full stretch on tummy – extend arms and legs as far as possible to make themselves really long.
Be careful how you crawl back out again – mind you don't bang your head.	Commando crawl – as before, but backwards.
We need to get our swimming things ready. Let's roll up our swimming costume in our towel so we don't lose it. Tuck it under your arm and come and put it in the bag.	High kneeling on the floor. Lean forwards and roll up towel, using both hands. Pick it up and place it under 1 arm. Walk forwards and put it in the bag.

SKILL

NARRATION	ACTION
Come on, pick up your bucket and spade and let's go and catch the bus!	The children should pick up their bucket and spade, 1 in each hand.
Let's go downstairs now.	The children walk forwards with high knees, as if going downstairs.
Let's close the front door behind us and off we go. Hold on tightly to your buckets and spades, and make sure you don't bump into anyone else.	The children walk forwards around the room, using all the space and without making contact with anyone else. They stop on the practitioner's command.
We need to turn down this road to get to the bus stop. Can you turn towards the hand holding the bucket?	The children all start walking again and 'turn a corner' before setting off again. If appropriate, the terms left and right may be used.
It feels as if the bucket is getting heavy. Can you swap your bucket and spade over and hold them with the other hand?	The children swap over the bucket and spade into the opposite hand. Encourage them to transfer at least 1 item without putting it down on the floor.
We are nearly there, but first we must go down this road. Can you turn towards the hand holding the bucket again?	The children should make another turn before setting off. Use the words left and right if appropriate.
At last we are at the bus stop. Put down your bucket and spade, and stand quietly to wait for the bus. Perhaps you can be thinking about what you are going to do on the beach.	The children stand in a line quietly, then lie down on the floor, relaxing and thinking about the seaside.

Week 2: The bus ride

Aims

🐚 To use different travelling actions

🐚 To achieve different body shapes

🐚 To develop pelvic strength

Equipment needed

☼ **Warm-up:** 2 buckets (or cones)

🦀 **Strength:** None

🐬 **Skill:** CD track 20: Seaside atmosphere

WARM-UP

NARRATION	ACTION
I can see the bus coming! Stand still so that you are ready.	The children should stand with 2 feet flat on the floor, arms by sides, trying to remain still.
Hooray! Hooray! Here's the bus! Isn't it exciting?	The children jump up in the air, taking off from 2 feet and stretching arms up, and shout 'Hooray!' Ask them to try landing on 2 feet.
Climb up the steps carefully so that you don't trip. Hold on to the rail.	The children move forwards, bringing their knees high, as if climbing stairs, and swinging their arms to reach the rails.
Move down the bus carefully – there isn't much room between the seats. You'll need to take tiny steps so that you don't bump into anyone.	The children move forwards slowly, taking small steps and keeping their arms tucked in and tight body shape.
Move right down the bus. There are seats for everyone.	The children walk on tiptoes between 2 upturned buckets (or cones) placed 3 m apart.

STRENGTH

NARRATION	ACTION
Let's find a seat. We'll have to turn and slide into it to sit down.	The children then turn round to face the opposite direction. They side step and sit down.
Let's try that again going the other way to help those children who are going to sit on the other side of the bus.	Repeat as above, but this time in the opposite direction.
We will have to sit still while the bus is moving. Off we go!	The children sit on the floor with knees bent up and feet flat on the floor. Hands are on the floor beside hips with fingers facing forwards.
Oh, this is a bumpy ride! Can you feel your bottom lifting off the seat?	The children lift their bottoms off the floor and push hips forwards without moving hands, as if going over bumps.
Goodness, now we're going round some bends! First 1 way – then the other! Hold tight!	Still in the same position, the children lean over to 1 side, lifting 1 hip off the floor, then back to the other side.

SKILL

NARRATION	ACTION
Hooray! We've arrived at the seaside. Can you see the sea? Look both ways and you'll find it. We'll have to shield our eyes from the sun.	Still sitting, the children lift 1 hand and place it above their eyes to shield them from the sun. Then they turn their heads to look from side to side, taking their hand across the midline. Repeat with the other hand.
The bus has stopped and it is time to get off. Stand up carefully and slide your way across the seat.	The children should roll over on to their knees and try to stand up without using their hands to push up, then side step to move into the aisle – in both directions as before.
Oh dear! The driver has parked on a bit of a slope. Be careful how you get off as it's very wobbly.	Moving very slowly forwards, but wobbling from side to side as they move – taking 1 or 2 steps to each side. Then 2 big steps to go down the stairs.
Let's hurry to the beach – we're going to have great fun. Can you run? Not too fast though – we don't want any accidents.	Running in all directions, taking care not to bump into others.
Now that we've got to the beach, it's time to lie down and have a rest for a few moments. We've had a very exhausting journey.	The children lie on the floor and pretend to go to sleep.

Week 3: Safe in the sun

Aims

- Revision of different travelling actions
- To develop shoulder strength
- To learn new travelling actions

Equipment needed

- **Warm-up:** None
- **Strength:** Parachute or large blanket
- **Skill:** Parachute or large blanket; CD track 20: Seaside atmosphere

WARM-UP

NARRATION	ACTION
Now that we've got to the beach we must find somewhere comfortable to sit.	The children move forwards, walking at a brisk pace.
There are a lot of pebbles on this part of the beach. We'll have to walk on tiptoes so as not to hurt our feet.	They then move on to tiptoes, walking slowly and stooping down as if on pebbles.
Now we've come to some wet sand. This is difficult to walk in, isn't it, as our feet get stuck? This isn't the right place to sit either.	The children walk as if in wet sand, lifting their knees up high and pulling their feet up.
Here's a little stream. Can you run and jump over it?	The children run and jump, 1-footed take-off.
I can see just the place for us to go, over there by that rock. Quick, let's run to get there before someone else does. Stop and sit down quickly when I call.	The children run around the room, stop quickly and sit down.

STRENGTH

NARRATION	ACTION
This is just the right place to put our blanket. Let's shake out our blanket so that we can put it down to sit on. It will be safer for us and more comfortable than sitting on the sand. Each of you take hold of a corner.	Using either a parachute or a large blanket, let the children each hold a corner or the edge, with both hands and arms outstretched.
Let's give it a good shake now. Can you lift it up in the air first? Well done – now bring it back down to your knees again. Keep holding on tightly. We don't want it to blow away!	The children lift the parachute/blanket up as high as they can, then bring it back down again, keeping their arms outstretched and bending their knees.
We'll do that again, 3 times, to make sure it's ready for us to sit down.	Repeat as above, 3 times.
Right, now let's put it down on the ground. Don't forget to bend your knees as you take it down.	All bend down and place the parachute/blanket on the floor.

SKILL

NARRATION	ACTION
I can't find my bag – I think it must be under the blanket. You'll have to take turns to crawl underneath to find it for me. The rest of us will hold the blanket up while you have your turn at crawling.	The children each crawl from 1 side of the parachute/blanket to the other on hands and knees in turn. The others lift it up to knee height.
Well done, you were very good at that. Could you now try sliding on your tummies to get to the other side?	Using hands to propel themselves, the children slide underneath the parachute/blanket from 1 side to another.
Oh, my bag was over there all the time and not under the blanket! But now there seem to be a few wrinkles in our blanket and that won't be very comfortable to sit on. Let's have a go at rolling on it to smooth it out.	This time on top of the parachute/blanket, the children roll over and over using extended arms and legs (log rolls), making sure they go in both directions.
That looks better. Now it's ready for us to use. You must be very tired after all that shaking. Perhaps you should lie down and have a rest. Can you curl up really small this time so that there is room for everyone on the blanket?	The children lie down on the parachute/blanket and curl up as small as possible.

Week 4: Paddling in the sea

Aims

🐚 To travel in different directions

🐚 To achieve a simple balance

🐚 To perform simple jumps

Equipment needed

☀ **Warm-up:** None

🦀 **Strength:** None

🐬 **Skill:** CD track 20: Seaside atmosphere

WARM-UP

NARRATION	ACTION
I think it's time we went to paddle in the sea. It will cool us down. The sand feels quite hot under our feet, so we'll have to run on tiptoe to get to the water's edge quickly.	The children run about the room on tiptoe.
Here the sand is quite wet as we get nearer to the sea. Can you take great big steps and stamp your feet to make footprints in the sand?	The children lift their knees high and stamp with flat feet as if to make an imprint in the sand.
We're here now at the water's edge. Oh, the water is freezing. Quickly run away from the waves as they break on the beach, so they can't catch you.	The children run forwards and then away as they are told that another wave is breaking. Those who can should try running backwards. Repeat this several times.

STRENGTH

NARRATION	ACTION
Oh, look at that dog over there. He's having great fun on the beach. Can you pretend to be a dog and walk on your hands and feet? You'll have to bend your knees a little.	The children walk on hands and feet, going in different directions.
The dog is going to the water's edge. The water is tickling his toes. He'll have to lift up his paw to keep it from getting wet. Can you lift 1 leg off the floor like the dog? Now try the other.	The children hold the balance on 2 hands and 1 foot. Make sure they try on both sides.
Oh, now the dog is lifting 2 paws at the same time – 1 of his front paws and 1 of his back paws. Do you think you could do that without falling over?	The children should try lifting a hand and a foot from the floor at the same time. If possible see whether they can first lift diagonally opposite, then on the same side of the body.

SKILL

NARRATION	ACTION
Shall we have a go at jumping over the waves? Our feet have got a bit more used to the cold water now. To start with, let's try jumping from 2 feet and landing on 2 feet.	The children should bend their knees to push off and jump up in the air. Landing with feet apart is acceptable, although they should start with feet together.
Perhaps we could now try jumping from 1 leg and landing on the same leg. This is called hopping.	The children should have a go at hopping and will probably need to move forwards or turn round. They should then try to hop on the other leg.
Would you like to try jumping over the waves with a partner? Hold hands and jump over together. Try not to splash each other too much!	With a partner, the children should practise jumping together. They should try to jump up at the same time, so they may need help with the timing (e.g. counting or beating).
It feels good just to sit quietly at the edge of the water and let the waves break over our toes. Sometimes it tickles, so you may just want to wriggle your toes, but try to keep your legs still and relax.	The children sit quietly, with minimal movement and relaxed.

Gross motor week 4

35

Week 5: Building sandcastles

Aims

- To develop spatial awareness
- To develop shoulder strength
- To develop bilateral movement

Equipment needed

Warm-up: Buckets spaced around the room

Strength: Bucket and spade per child; song 14: Dig, dig, digging in the sand

Skill: Paddling pool filled with shredded paper, bucket and spade per child; CD track 20: Seaside atmosphere

WARM-UP

NARRATION	ACTION
There are lots of buckets on the beach. We must walk slowly to make sure we don't knock them over. Can you walk in and out of them?	The buckets are placed randomly around the room and the children walk in and out of them, avoiding the buckets and other children.
You seem to be very good at that. I wonder whether you could now go a little faster, but still without knocking any buckets over.	The children repeat the activity, now running in and out of the buckets.
This time when I call 'Stop', can you stop very quickly next to a bucket and keep very still?	The activity is repeated as above, but the children should be still and hold a balance when asked to stop beside any bucket.
Each of you has your own bucket. This time when I call 'Stop', could you find your own bucket, and keep still beside it?	Ensure that the children continue to use all the space around the room in which to move and do not remain in a small area around their own bucket.

STRENGTH

NARRATION	ACTION
We have all got our buckets. Now we need our spades so that we can do some digging and make sandcastles. They are over there. This time let's turn over with our bottoms down next to the floor and push along with our hands and feet, like this. Your bottoms will make a pattern in the sand as you move.	The children move by sliding their bottoms between the buckets along the floor, using hands and feet to push. (A demonstration may be required!) Try to get them to think about the pathway they are travelling, so they imagine the mark they would leave in the sand.
Let's go back to our buckets now. Move along on your bottom as before, and then you will be able to balance your spade on your lap to carry it.	The children should manage to balance their spades on their laps as they travel.
Shall we start to build a sandcastle? You'll have to dig lots of sand to make a nice big one. Can you practise digging now? We'll sing while we are digging.	Making sure they have plenty of space, the children use their spades to do some imaginary digging. Encourage them to use large movements, with the digging action going up to shoulder level.
I wonder whether you can be really clever and dig on the other side now?	The children should swap their hands over, so the other hand is now at the top. Digging action is now on the other side of their bodies.

SKILL

NARRATION	ACTION
Now we are going to scoop up this paper with our hands and pretend to build sandcastles. Use 2 hands to fill up your bucket. When it is full, turn it upside down, and pat it with your spade.	Using shredded paper, the children should fill their buckets using large scooping movements with both hands at once. They should try to turn the bucket quickly, so as not to lose too much paper. Then use their spades to tap the bottom of their upturned buckets, before lifting them.
It's good fun to make sandcastles but it's also good fun to knock them down. Can you jump on your sandcastle to squash it?	The children jump on their sandcastle.
Let's make 1 great big sandcastle that we can all jump on. Can you collect up your paper and put it back in the paddling pool? Then we will all have a turn at jumping in it.	The children collect up their paper, and put it back in the paddling pool. Then, 2 at a time, they have a go at jumping up and down in the paddling pool.
We're worn out knocking down all those sandcastles. I think it is time to have a rest before we play some more games on the beach. It's time to lie down and rest and keep very still.	The children lie down and relax, taking up whichever position they prefer, but keeping very still.

Week 6: Having a picnic

Aims

- To develop spatial and directional awareness
- To experience balance and achieve more body awareness
- To develop shoulder strength and flexibility

Equipment needed

Warm-up: None

Strength: None

Skill: Parachute or large blanket

WARM-UP

NARRATION	ACTION
This is a lovely beach! The sand stretches a really long way. Let's look at the different things on the beach. We'll start off walking forwards.	The children walk forwards, as if looking at different things (e.g. rocks, seaweed, shells).
Now we're going to try walking in some different directions. Listen to my voice to find out which way you should go.	Ask the children to try walking in different directions (e.g. backwards, forwards and sideways). Ensure that they have a turn in both directions – they may find this difficult.
You're getting really good at that. We'll be able to try it running now. Do you think you can run in lots of different directions?	As above, but now speeding up. Make sure that the children remain well spaced, to avoid collisions.

STRENGTH

NARRATION	ACTION
Oh, look at those seagulls! They're standing on 1 leg! Can you stand on 1 leg like them? Have a go at lifting 1 foot off the floor behind you. You may want to stretch your arms out to the sides to help you, a bit like the seagulls' wings.	Encourage the children to lift 1 leg off the floor, bending the knee and lifting the foot behind them. They may need to start off by holding on to the wall if they cannot achieve this otherwise.
Can you stand on the other leg now? I don't think seagulls always stand on the same leg.	Standing on the other leg. Some children may be unaware of which leg they used for balance the first time, so you may need to develop a strategy to help with this.
They're very greedy birds – I think they may be hoping for some of our food. I don't think we want them near us while we're having our picnic. Let's run and clap our hands and chase them away. There are lots of them, so we'll have to do lots of clapping.	The children run around the room clapping hands in lots of different spaces (e.g. high, low, to the side, in front).

SKILL

NARRATION	ACTION
Now that it is time for our picnic, we need to spread out the blanket, so we can all sit down. Can you all help with this? Each take hold of an edge of the blanket.	Using a blanket or parachute, make sure each child takes hold of an edge or handle with both hands.
Everyone start off close together. Now walk backwards away from each other. Hold on tightly to the blanket.	The children get together in a tight group with the parachute/blanket between them, then move backwards, gradually unfolding it.
Now we're going to move to the side to make sure we get rid of all the creases. We're going to go this way first – to the right. Everyone watch me to see which way to go.	Still holding on with 2 hands, the children side step to the right.
Now we're going back the other way, to the left.	Side stepping to the left.
That's it. We're nearly ready to put the blanket down on the ground. Let's give it a last shake. Everyone walk forwards and lift the blanket high. Now backwards and bend down and put it gently on the floor. Hooray – now we're ready for our picnic. Sit down nicely on the blanket to show everyone you are ready.	As in Simon Says, holding the parachute/blanket, the children walk forwards and lift their arms up above their heads. Then they walk backwards, gradually bringing their arms down, bending their knees and laying the parachute/blanket down on the ground. It would be a lovely idea for the children to finish the session by having a snack sitting on it.

Week 7: What's in the rock pools?

Aims

 To reinforce and revise work on spatial awareness

 To develop reciprocal movement

 To develop pelvic and shoulder strength

Equipment needed

Warm-up: 1 plastic hoop per child

Strength: None

Skill: 1 plastic hoop per child, 1 beanbag per child; CD track 20: Seaside atmosphere

WARM-UP

NARRATION	ACTION
Over here there are lots of rock pools. Let's run in and out of them. Be careful not to slip as the rocks may be quite wet and slippery.	Hoops are laid out on the floor. The children run in and out of them, taking care not to slip.
Let's dip our toes in the water and see how warm the water is. Oh, it's not very warm! Shake your toes to get them dry.	The children step up to the hoops and dip their toes in, 1 foot at a time. They then shake that foot, before trying with the other.
Now we'll step into the rock pools. Oh, it's really cold. Step out backwards again carefully. Can you try that again, this time with the other foot going in and out again first?	The children step into hoops, first 1 foot, then the other. With the same foot leading, they then step backwards out again. Repeat, leading with the other foot.
I can see a little creature in the water. Can you see that starfish? Perhaps you can lie on the floor and pretend to be a starfish – you'll have to stretch your arms and legs out really wide.	The children lie on their backs on the floor, making a star shape.
Oh, look – there's another starfish, but that one is on its side. Can you stand up and make a star shape to look like it? Starfish are very stiff and don't move much.	Taking up a very wide base, the children stretch out into a star shape, keeping their heads up.

Gross motor week 7

STRENGTH

NARRATION	ACTION
Can you see the little fish swimming in the rock pool? They swim about like this, wiggling their bodies from side to side.	The children commando crawl – lying on their tummy and using arms to pull their body along, with legs remaining still.
There are some little crabs in the pools too. They walk like this.	The children now sit on the floor, with feet flat on floor and hands placed beside the hips. They lift their bottoms off the floor, point their tummies to the ceiling and walk on hands and feet. Make sure that chins are kept down on the chest.
Those seagulls are there again. I think they are watching the fish swimming about. This time they are jumping, from 2 feet to 2 feet. Perhaps you can jump like them 3 times.	Standing jumps, taking off from 2 feet and landing on 2 feet, trying to put 3 into a sequence.
Those seagulls are hopping on 1 leg. Can you do that? Now try hopping on the other leg.	Encourage the children to travel while hopping, trying to do several in succession.

SKILL

NARRATION	ACTION
Let's find a pebble and throw it into the rock pool. Listen to the splash!	The children each have a beanbag and throw it into their hoop.
Find some more pebbles and have another go. See how many you can throw into the water.	Each has 5 tries at throwing beanbags into the hoop, counting how many they score.
I think we must have disturbed a jellyfish with our pebbles. It moves by wiggling along. It's not stiff like the starfish but all floppy. Can you wiggle like a jelly fish?	The children stand and with arms outstretched, wiggle down through their bodies to their toes, this time being very floppy.
There are some very tiny crabs that you can hardly see as they are so small. Can you pretend to be a tiny little crab and curl up really small on the floor and go to sleep? You'll have to hug your knees really tightly.	The children curl up as small as they can, on their backs, on their tummies or on their sides. They pretend to go to sleep.

Week 8: Playing games on the beach

Aims

- To develop spatial awareness
- To increase trunk stability
- To develop early ball-handling skills

Equipment needed

Warm-up: Ribbon or band per child

Strength: None

Skill: Ball; CD track 20: Seaside atmosphere

WARM-UP

NARRATION	ACTION
There's lots of seaweed on the beach. We're going to see how much we can collect.	Each child has a ribbon or band, which they tuck into the back of their waistband. The practitioner starts by walking and seeing how many bands they can collect, with the children also walking.
Now one of you is going to collect the seaweed.	Same activity, but with a child now collecting the bands. When appropriate, 2 children could collect at the same time.
Now we'll try going a little bit faster. We're still coming round trying to collect seaweed, though!	If appropriate, move on to running to collect the bands.
All of you are going to collect seaweed now. You have to try and get your partner's!	In 2s, each trying to take hold of their partner's band.

STRENGTH

NARRATION	ACTION
I'm going to make a bridge on the beach, and make it really strong. I wonder whether you could push it over?	Yourself on all 4s, ask children to try pushing you over. Let them feel how strong you are.
Now we're going to see if you can make strong bridges just like mine.	In 2s, 1 makes a bridge, and the other tries to push them over, then the children swap over. They can try on hands and knees and hands and feet. Try to pair children of similar size.
I wonder whether you might be able to crawl through each other's bridges? You'll have to crawl on your tummies to get through.	1 child holds a bridge position, this time on hands and feet, with bottom high. Other child commando crawls underneath, going from 1 side to the other, not from head to foot.

SKILL

NARRATION	ACTION
Ball games on the beach are great fun. We'll start off with an easy game. Can you join hands in a circle?	In a small circle, maximum of 8 children, pass the ball around in a clockwise direction, then anti-clockwise. Encourage the children to cross the midline on both sides.
Now we're going to play some more ball games. Sit down on the sand with your friends, but this time we're going to split into 2 groups. We'll see whether you are good at rolling and stopping the ball.	In 4s, children sit on the floor with legs wide, starting fairly close. They roll the ball to each other with 2 hands, stopping before sending it back again. They gradually move further away from each other as they improve. Then they could try high kneeling or half kneeling to roll the ball.
Now we're going to play a team ball game. Can you stand in a line, 1 behind the other in your little group?	In 4s, children stand behind each other, with legs wide. The child at the front rolls the ball through the tunnel. The child at the back collects the ball, takes it to the front and continues. Repeat until the children are back in their original positions.
It's been fun playing games on the beach, but it's very tiring. I think we need to lie down and have a rest. Can you lie down on your backs with your legs and arms spread wide like the starfish? Now change into a long thin shape, like a strip of seaweed. Can you remember curling up really small like the little crab?	The children lie down on the floor and listen to your voice, taking up the different positions with their bodies.

Week 9: Didn't we have a lovely time at the seaside?

Aims

🐚 To develop balancing skills

🐚 To work co-operatively within a group

🐚 To develop ball skills

Equipment needed

☀ **Warm-up:** 1 coloured spot per child

🦀 **Strength:** 1 coloured spot per child

🐬 **Skill:** Large ball, airflow ball, small bat / cardboard tube, cone;
CD track 20: Seaside atmosphere

WARM-UP

NARRATION	ACTION
Now it's nearly time to go home, I think we can knock down our sandcastles. Shall we jump on them?	Jumping on to a coloured spot, 2 feet to 2 feet, in 4 different directions.
Do you remember that seagull? He's come to stand where we've knocked our sandcastle down. Can you stand like him? Oh, look – now he's hopping!	The children try to stand on 1 leg on the spot, then try hopping on the spot. Ensure the children try to hop on both legs.
I think the seagull is just about to fly away. Can you see how he is stretching up and spreading his wings as if he is going to take off?	On the spot, the children stretch up, standing on their toes, and stretch out their arms to the sides.
There he goes. Let's run and flap our wings like the seagull.	The children run on tiptoe, flapping arms up and down as they run.

STRENGTH

NARRATION	ACTION
You were really good at balancing on 1 leg like the seagull. Let's try balancing on some other parts of your body now.	Again using the spots, ask children to achieve 'moments of stillness' using varied body parts (e.g. hands and feet, hands and knees, hands and seats).
I think you might be able to balance on an even smaller part of your body. Try lifting 1 hand or 1 foot off the floor.	Now into 3-point balancing, prone and supine (e.g. 3-point bridge).
We've had some good fun at the beach. Shall we have a race now? You're going to crawl on the sand and try to beat your partner.	Commando crawling, in 2s, going in the same direction.

SKILL

NARRATION	ACTION
We enjoyed playing games on the beach. Let's play some more before it's time to go home. I wonder whether you are good at kicking the ball? Football on the beach is great fun.	In a small circle, the children kick across the circle to another child, starting with a static ball each time.
Let's try that with 1 person standing in the middle of the circle kicking to everyone in turn.	The practitioner stands in the middle of the circle and kicks to each child in turn, who then kicks it back to the middle.
You were so good! We'll try the same thing throwing the ball now.	Repeat as above, but this time with gentle throws.
I wonder whether you're good at hitting a ball too? Take the bat and hit the ball off the top of the cone.	Place a small ball (e.g. airflow) on top of a cone. Each child has a turn at hitting it off, using a small bat or cardboard tube or similar implement.
I'm afraid it's time to go home now. Let's make sure we pick up all our belongings – we don't want to leave any behind.	The children walk round slowly, picking up all of the spots, balls, etc. and putting them away.
We've had a lovely day and have been very busy. You must be really tired now. Let's have a lie down before we start our journey home.	The children lie down on the floor and relax.

Fine motor sessions

Week 1: Getting ready

Session A

☀ **Warm-up:** Standing

🦀 **Activity:** Play dough towels

Aims

📷 To develop hand co-ordination skills

📷 To cross the midline

Equipment needed

♪ **Song 1:** I have two eyes to see with

♪ **Song 2:** Pat yourself on the back

🐚 Enough play dough for each child to make a rolled-up towel, large bag

NARRATION	WARM-UP
It's time to open your eyes and wake up – it's the day we're going to the seaside!	Children sing Song 1: I have two eyes to see with.
Let's wake ourselves up a bit more by stretching up as far as we can.	The children stand and stretch their arms straight up above their heads as far as they can.
We need to wash our faces. Make sure you wash your nose, round your mouth and round your eyes.	The children pretend to take a flannel and wash their faces.
Now we need to get fit for the journey, so first we must warm up our arms and shoulders.	The children pat themselves on their backs. Take right hand over left shoulder and then left hand over right shoulder. Children sing Song 2: Pat yourself on the back.

NARRATION	ACTIVITY
We must get our swimming things ready to take to the seaside. Can you roll up your towel ready to put in the bag? Use both hands to do this.	Using play dough, the children make roly-poly/sausage shapes. Encourage them to make rolls of differing shapes and sizes. The rolled towels can then be placed in a bag in the centre of the table.

Session B

 Warm-up: Standing, then sitting on a chair

 Activity: Buying a ticket

Aim

 To develop hand–eye co-ordination

Equipment needed

 Song 2: Pat yourself on the back

Buckets, small spades, large spoons, ladles, rice, pasta, etc.

NARRATION	WARM-UP
When we are at the seaside we shall go on the beach. We must find our buckets and spades to make some sandcastles. Are they on top of the wardrobe? Make sure you hold on to them tightly.	The children stand and stretch their arms straight up above their heads as far as they can. They clench their fists tightly, then open them again as if gripping the handles of a bucket and spade.
I hope your shoulders and arms are not too tired after all that stretching! Let's try shaking our arms, first 1, then the other.	The children hold 1 arm up in front or out to the side and shake it loosely. They repeat with the other arm.
Well done – you got those buckets and spades down really carefully. Give yourselves a pat on the back!	The children pat themselves on their backs. Take right hand over left shoulder and then left hand over right shoulder. Children sing Song 2: Pat yourself on the back.

NARRATION	ACTIVITY
We had better practise shovelling the sand so that you can make some big sandcastles. Can you use your spade to fill your bucket?	In the sand tray children practise spooning and shovelling to fill their buckets. This can also be practised using large spoons with rice, pasta, etc.

Fine motor week 1

Session C

☀ **Warm-up:** Standing, then sitting on a chair

🦀 **Activity:** Putting coins in a purse

Aims

 To develop hand–eye co-ordination

 To develop bilateral skills

Equipment needed

♫ **Song 3:** Hello

♫ **Song 4:** Bottom back, feet flat

♫ **Song 5:** This is the way we wait for the bus

🐚 1 purse and 10 coins per child

NARRATION	WARM-UP
We're going to the seaside with our friends. We're going to walk to the bus stop to meet them. Let's say 'Hello' to them.	The children wave hands to the other children. Then they shake hands with a partner. They sing Song 3: Hello.
We're really excited to be going to the seaside. Let's show everyone how happy we are.	The children jump up in the air, taking off from 2 feet and stretching arms up, and shout 'Hooray!'
Let's sing a song while we are waiting for the bus to arrive. Make sure you are sitting nicely.	Children sing Song 4: Bottom back, feet flat.

NARRATION	ACTIVITY
We need to take some pocket money with us to buy ice cream at the seaside. Get your coins and put them safely in your own purse.	The children take 10 coins out of a box, 1 at a time, using only 1 hand and counting as they do so. They put the coins in their own purse, which they should hold in the other hand. Then they fasten the purse securely.
Oh dear! The bus still hasn't arrived. Let's sing another song while we are waiting.	Children sing Song 5: This is the way we wait for the bus.

Week 2: The bus ride

Session A

☼ **Warm-up:** Standing, then sitting on a chair

🦀 **Activity:** Buying a ticket

Aims

📷 To develop pincer grip

📷 To develop finger strength

Equipment needed

🎵 **Song 4:** Bottom back, feet flat

🎵 **Song 6:** The big red bus

🐚 Purse containing 10 coins for each child, book of cloakroom tickets

NARRATION	WARM-UP
Here comes the bus. Put out your arm to make sure the driver knows we want to get on.	The children stand with arms by sides, and lift up 1 arm to horizontal position. Then repeat on the other side.
The bus is about to move. Sit very still. Let's sing our song.	Children sing Song 4: Bottom back, feet flat.
Goodness me, this ride is very bumpy! Can you feel your bottom lifting off the seat?	The children should put their hands on the sides of the seat, feet flat on the floor and facing forwards. They lift their bottoms up and down off the seat, without losing contact with their hands.
Let's sing a song about our bumpy ride!	Children sing Song 6: The big red bus.
Now the bus is going along a very bendy road! Make sure you are sitting properly and holding on tight.	The children hold on to the sides of their seats and lean over from one side to the other.

NARRATION	ACTIVITY
We shall have to buy a ticket to travel on this bus. Can you find the money in your purse to pay for it?	The children each open their purse, take a coin out of it, and exchange it for a ticket, which they have to tear off a strip. They then put the ticket in their own purse.

Session B

 Warm-up: Standing, then sitting on a chair

 Activity: Drawing large circles

Aim

 To develop shoulder strength and mobility

Equipment needed

 Song 7: The wheels on the bus

 Paper on easel or raised board, whiteboard or blackboard, pencils and crayons, playground chalk

NARRATION	WARM-UP
This bus has lots of great big wheels. Can you draw the shape of the wheels in the air?	The children stand in a space and trace large circles in the air with one hand. Ensure that the movements are whole arm movements, originating from the shoulder. Repeat with the other arm.
We know a song about the wheels on a bus. Let's sing it now.	Children sing Song 7: The wheels on the bus.
Sometimes when it is raining, the driver needs to use windscreen wipers. Can you show me how they work?	Standing facing forwards, the children move both arms together in a swaying movement, trying to get full mobility in the shoulders.
There are a lot of people waving to us as we drive past. We can wave back to them.	The children sit down and wave to the other children in the class, ensuring wrist mobility.
NARRATION	**ACTIVITY**
We are going to draw pictures of those great big wheels on the bus. Do you know how many wheels they have?	Drawing large circles, on to paper pinned on an easel or on a whiteboard or blackboard, or chalk on the playground.

Fine motor week 2

Session C

 Warm-up: Standing, then sitting on a chair

 Activity: Painting a picture of a bus

Aim

 To develop shoulder strength and flexibility

Equipment needed

 Purse for each child, bucket and spade per child, large paintbrush per child, large sheets of paper/boxes, etc. to make bus

NARRATION	WARM-UP
At last we have arrived at the seaside. We will need to make sure we don't leave anything behind on the bus when we get off. Pick up your purse and bucket and spade.	While still sitting the children should reach down to the floor, first on 1 side and then the other, to pick up their belongings.
Despite the bumpy ride, the driver has got us all here safely. I think we should shake his hand and say 'Thank you' as we get off the bus.	Working with a partner, the children shake 1 hand at a time, both hands in turn, to a count of 3 each time. They start off with arms straight, and then with arms crossed diagonally. Again to a count of 3, the children grasp both hands and shake, first with arms straight, then with arms crossed diagonally, and say 'Thank you'.

NARRATION	ACTIVITY
Today we are going to paint a picture of a bus – just like the one that is taking us for our day at the seaside. We are going to use big brushes to paint.	The children each paint their own part of the bus, using large brushes (encouraging large arm movements). These may contribute towards painting a large picture, a 3D bus made out of boxes, or whatever best suits the setting.

Week 3: Safe in the sun

Session A

 Warm-up: Standing

 Activity: Water bottle exercises

Aims

 To develop shoulder and arm strength

 To develop co-ordination

Equipment needed

 Song 2: Pat yourself on the back

One water bottle per child

NARRATION	WARM-UP
Do you remember that we were very tired after our bus ride and we lay down to have a rest? I think we need to have a good stretch now that we're ready to enjoy ourselves.	The children stand and stretch their arms straight up above their heads as far as they can.
It's really exciting being on the beach. Let's jump and show everyone how pleased we are to be here.	The children jump up in the air, taking off from 2 feet and stretching arms up, and shout 'Hooray!'
While we are on the beach we are going to do some digging in the sand. We had better warm up our arms and shoulders so that we are ready.	The children pat themselves on the back. Take right hand over left shoulder and then left hand over right shoulder. Children sing Song 2: Pat yourself on the back.

NARRATION	ACTIVITY
We shall need to drink plenty of water when we are in the hot sun. Can you hold your bottle of water?	**1.** Each child stands beside their chair, holding a bottle of water in 1 hand; this arm should be bent, bringing the bottle up to the shoulder, then lifting it up above the head. Change hands and repeat with the other arm. **2.** Holding bottle in the first hand again, stretch arm out to side. Bring bottle in beside the face and back out again. Change hands and repeat. A song may be sung as the activities are carried out.

Fine motor week 3

Session B

Warm-up: Standing

Activity: Decorating sun hats

Aims

To develop bilateral skills

To develop pencil skills

Equipment needed

Song 3: Hello

Song 8: Wear your sun hat

One paper hat with a peak per child, crayons

NARRATION	WARM-UP
All of our friends have come with us to the seaside. Let's say 'Hello' to them again and sing our song.	The children wave hands to the other children or shake hands with a partner. They then sing Song 3: Hello.
We are going to wear hats on the beach to protect our heads from the sun. Can you practise putting a hat on and lifting it off again? Press your hands down flat on your head and then stretch them up in the air again.	The children should press lightly down on the tops of their heads with both hands, elbows bent and out to the sides. Then the arms should be extended above the head. Repeat several times.
Let's sing a song about wearing our sun hats.	Children sing Song 8: Wear your sun hat.

NARRATION	ACTIVITY
We are going to decorate our sun hats to make them look really colourful. Then we shall be able to wear them on the beach. Can you draw a picture of the sun on the front of your hat?	Each child is given a paper hat. They decorate it using crayons, including drawing the sun on the peak.

Session C

 Warm-up: Standing

 Activity: Rubbing on sun cream

Aims

 To develop wrist flexibility and strength

 To encourage body awareness (proprioceptive skills)

Equipment needed

 Song 9: This is the way we wash our hands

 Song 10: The sun cream song

One screw-top bottle and lid per child

NARRATION	WARM-UP
The sun is shining. We must put some sun cream on our skin so we do not get sun burnt. First we must make sure our hands are ready to put on the cream. We will go to the stream and wash them in the water.	The children rub hands together, as if washing them. They sing Song 9: This is the way we wash our hands.
Let's dry our hands by shaking them to get the water off.	The children shake both hands, demonstrating flexibility in the wrists and keeping the hands loose.
Now we need to make sure our hands are firm to rub in the sun cream.	Hand presses. Place hands together, elbows out, and push hands together for a count of 10.

NARRATION	ACTIVITY
The sun is very hot. We must now rub in the sun cream. Take the bottle, unscrew the lid and put some cream in your hand. Now rub it all over your body. When that hand gets tired, have a go with the other hand. We'll sing a song as we are doing it.	The children unscrew the lid and pretend to pour some cream into their hands, which they rub into different parts of their body, naming them in time to the song. They sing Song 10: The sun cream song.

Fine motor week 3

Week 4: Paddling in the sea

Session A

Warm-up: Standing

Activity: Drawing/painting the waves

Aims

To cross the midline

To develop pencil skills

Equipment needed

Song 11: Shake the blanket out

1 tea towel for each pair of children

Large sheet of paper per child (placed landscape), crayons, paints, paintbrushes.

NARRATION	WARM-UP
We're going to find somewhere comfortable to sit on the beach and spread our blanket. Let's warm up our arms and shoulders before we do that. Bring both arms up in front of you, then swing them back down past your knees and just behind you.	Standing in a space, the children swing arms backwards and forwards, bending the knees slightly as arms are lowered.
Now we're ready to shake the blanket. Lift your arms up in front and take hold of it with both hands. Hold on tightly while we shake it.	In pairs the children hold on to a 'blanket' (tea towel size) and shake it up and down.
I know a song we can sing while we are shaking. Let's sing it now.	Children sing Song 11: Shake the blanket out.

NARRATION	ACTIVITY
The sun is very hot, but the sea looks lovely and cool. There are lots of waves for jumping over. Can you draw a picture of the sea? You could draw lots of wavy lines.	Each child has a large piece of paper, which should be placed landscape on a table/easel. They should paint or draw a picture of the sea, being encouraged to draw long, flowing lines across the page and hopefully taking their hand across the midline.

Session B

 Warm-up: Sitting

 Activity: Drawing in the sand (fingers/toes)

Aims

 To develop finger/toe isolation skills

To encourage copying skills

Equipment needed

 Song 12: Wiggle your fingers

 Sand tray

NARRATION	WARM-UP
While we are on the beach it feels good to wiggle our fingers in the sand. Can you wiggle your fingers?	The children are sitting down. They hold both hands up and wiggle their fingers.
Wiggling your toes is fun too. Can you wiggle your toes?	Still seated, the children lift the toes on both feet from the floor and wiggle. (Shoes will need to be removed for this activity.)
It feels good to wiggle your fingers and toes in the water too. Can you do them all together?	The children wiggle all their fingers and toes.
We can sing a song to help us.	Children sing Song 12: Wiggle your fingers.

NARRATION	ACTIVITY
Now we're going to draw some patterns in the sand with our fingers. Look at the pictures, and see whether you can draw them in the sand.	Show the children simple patterns and shapes, and get them to copy these drawing in the sand. Encourage the children to try with different fingers and both hands.
You were really good at that. Do you think you can draw pictures with your toes now?	Ask the children to use their big toe on both feet to make shapes in the sand.

Fine motor week 4

Session C

 Warm-up: Standing

 Activity: Water play

Aim

 To develop hand–eye co-ordination

Equipment needed

♪ **Song 13:** Splishy splashy, splishy splashy

 Water tray, plastic toys, pouring utensils

NARRATION	WARM-UP
Now we're going to go paddling in the sea. I know a good song we can sing.	Children sing Song 13: Splishy splashy, splishy splashy.
Do you remember that dog we saw on the beach? Most dogs like to swim in the sea. Can you move your arms like the dog's front paws – in doggy paddle?	The children practise circular movement with their arms, as in doggy paddle.
If we go in the water a little further we shall have to use our arms to push the water away as it gets a bit deeper. Can you use your arms one at a time to push the water away from you?	Use alternate arm movements, as in wading.

NARRATION	ACTIVITY
We're going to pretend to make some waves in the water. Move your hands backwards to make some waves.	The children wave their hands backwards and forwards to make waves in the water tray.
Let's make some different sounds in the water, like plipping and plopping. Try dropping different toys into the water and swishing them around to see what sounds they make.	Use a variety of small toys. Encourage moving them around in the water tray.
Are you good at pouring? We're going to fill up the watering cans and see whether you can pour the water into your bucket.	Any toys with a spout may be used to help children to pour into a bucket. Encourage them to use 2 hands and lift 1 elbow when pouring.

Fine motor week 4

61

Week 5: Building sandcastles

Session A

 Warm-up: Sitting at table

 Activity: Making sandcastles

Aims

 To develop bilateral movements

 To improve hand and finger strength

Equipment needed

 Song 4: Bottom back, feet flat

Bucket and spade per child, shells, moulds

NARRATION	WARM-UP
This week we're going to build some sandcastles. First we'll have to make sure our hands are ready to do lots of digging. Let's make sure we are sitting nicely – do you remember our song about good sitting?	The children sit on their chairs and sing Song 4: Bottom back, feet flat.
Can you rest your elbows on the table with hands in the air and press your hands together?	Elbows resting on the table, fingers pointing upwards, palms pressed together.
Now try lifting your elbows off the table and press your hands together. Press hard.	Elbows are lifted upwards and sideways, so that the forearms are parallel to the table.

NARRATION	ACTIVITY
Now we're ready to build our sandcastles. Pick up your buckets and spades and let's see what you can make.	The children use their spades to fill their buckets, and then make sandcastles.
We've got some shells to decorate your sandcastles. Can you pick them up 1 at a time and press them into the sand to make patterns?	Picking shells out of a bucket 1 at a time, the children use them to decorate their sandcastles.
Here are some other shapes that you can make in the sand. Perhaps you could use your hands this time to scoop up the sand. You may use shells to decorate them too.	The children fill a selection of moulds, this time using their hands to make different shapes in the sand.

Fine motor week 5

Session B

 Warm-up: Sitting at table

 Activity: Decorating flags

Aims

 To improve pencil skills

 To improve finger strength

Equipment needed

 Song 14: Dig, dig, digging in the sand

 Photocopiable 4 (p. 77) with flag shape (copied on to both sides of the paper) and straw per child, crayons, glue

NARRATION	WARM-UP
Do you remember digging in the sand? Let's sing the song about digging.	Children sing Song 14: Dig, dig, digging in the sand.
When we build sandcastles, we have to pat them to make them firm, so they don't crumble.	The children again sing Song 14: Dig, dig, digging in the sand.
Let's try some other things that we can do with our hands when we are building sandcastles. We can knead, like this. We can scrunch. We can squeeze.	The children copy the different actions, imagining that they are playing in the sand.
Sometimes we may need to make little holes in the sand to make windows in our castles. Can you press down on the table with your fingers 1 at a time, as if you are poking a hole in the sand?	Starting with their thumbs, the children tap the table several times, as if poking a hole in the sand. They then try the 2 index fingers, and so on.

NARRATION	ACTIVITY
Do you remember building sandcastles and decorating them with shells? Today we are going to make some flags that we can stick on our sandcastles. You are going to choose what colour you would like your flag to be.	Each child is given a copy of Photocopiable 4, with flag shapes printed on both sides. They colour in the shape they choose on both sides, and then tear round the outline. They then fix the flag to a pre-glued straw by rolling the paper around it.
We'll have to leave the flags to dry a little before we stick them in the sand.	

Fine motor week 5

Session C

 Warm-up: Standing or sitting

 Activity: Filling shapes in the sand

Aims

 To develop wrist mobility

 To improve pincer grip

Equipment needed

 Sand moulds, variety of spoons, colanders, jugs, funnels, etc., shells

NARRATION	WARM-UP
It feels good to have sand running through your fingers. Can you wiggle all of your fingers and pretend to feel the sand?	Using both hands the children move all of their fingers independently, as if sand is trickling through them.
Do you remember making different shapes in the sand with the moulds? We used our hands to fill them with sand. Let's pretend that we are using a spoon to put the sand in this time. When we play in the sand in a moment, you can try this properly.	The children should pretend to spoon, hopefully achieving rotation in their wrists.

NARRATION	ACTIVITY
Now you can try spooning into the moulds. You may be able to spoon only a little bit of sand at a time, so it will take you a bit longer to fill them this time.	Spooning into the sand moulds, using a variety of different sized and shaped spoons.
We have lots of other things that you can try filling with sand. Some of them have holes in, so you will be able to watch the sand trickling through.	Different utensils may be used in the sand – sieves, colanders, funnels, etc.
There are lots of shells hidden in the sand. Can you find each one and put them into the box? You will have to use your hands to dig in the sand.	Shells should be hidden in the sand, and the children hunt for them using only their hands. Encourage them to use a pincer grip to pick them up.

Fine motor week 5

Week 6: Having a picnic

Session A

☀ **Warm-up:** Standing

🦀 **Activity:** Preparing drinks

Aims

📷 To improve hand–eye co-ordination

📷 To improve hand and wrist strength and flexibility

Equipment needed

🎵 **Song 15:** Two fat seagulls

🐚 Water tray, jugs, cups, screw-top bottles and lids, straws

NARRATION	WARM-UP
Have you seen the seagulls on the beach? There are big mummy and daddy seagulls and little baby ones. When they are flying the big mummy and daddy seagulls flap their wings like this. Can you do that?	Holding both hands up in front, the children wave their hands up and down, trying to achieve good flexibility in their wrists.
The baby seagulls are just learning to fly. Their wings are much smaller, and look like this. See whether you can pretend to be the baby seagulls.	Still holding their hands up in front, this time the children keep their wrists still but wiggle all of their fingers up and down.
We can sing a song about seagulls.	Children sing Song 15: Two fat seagulls.

NARRATION	ACTIVITY
We're going to have a drink with our picnic. We had better practise pouring some water out of the jug.	In the water tray, practise pouring water from the jug into several cups.
Some people have brought bottles of drink, and we need to unscrew the tops and put a straw in for them.	They each have a turn at unscrewing the caps on 3 or 4 bottles, and inserting a straw in each.

Fine motor week 6

65

Session B

 Warm-up: Sitting on chairs

 Activity: Pass the food parcel

Aim

 To cross the midline

Equipment needed

 Song 4: Bottom back, feet flat

 Seaside medley (track 19)

Parcel wrapped with at least 1 layer for each child, including a small packet of raisins between each layer, band for each child to wear on one wrist

NARRATION	WARM-UP
When we sit down to eat our picnic we'll have to remember to sit nicely. Can you remember our song?	Sitting on their chairs the children sing Song 4: Bottom back, feet flat.
Do you remember the baby seagulls? They are really cute, aren't they? I think there is 1 on your shoulder. Can you reach across and stroke it with the opposite hand, like this?	The children take a hand across diagonally to stroke their opposite shoulder.
Oh no! It has jumped on your other shoulder! You'll have to change hands and stroke it on the other side.	Change hands and repeat.
You have done well! Can you reach across with both hands at the same time and give yourselves a pat on the back?	Take both hands diagonally across to the opposite shoulders, and pat on the back.

NARRATION	ACTIVITY
We've brought some food to have for our picnic. It's really well wrapped up in a packet. You'll all have to help us unwrap it. Can you sit in a circle? We'll pass the packet round. We'll listen to some seaside music while we're doing this, and each time the music stops the person holding the packet must take off a layer.	Pass the parcel, with 1 layer for each child. Encourage the children to give and receive the parcel with the same hand, thus crossing the midline. Change direction and ask them to use the other hand – they may need to wear something on 1 wrist to remind themselves which hand to use. At the end of the game the children may open their packets of raisins and eat them.

Fine motor week 6

Session C

 Warm-up: Sitting on chairs

 Activity: Making sandwiches

Aims

 To develop finger isolation

 To develop finger manipulation

Equipment needed

 Song 4: Bottom back, feet flat

 Slices of bread, banana, honey twizzler per child, honey, soft spread, plates, bowls and knives

NARRATION	WARM-UP
Are you ready for our picnic? Make sure you are sitting nicely. Let's sing our song again.	Children sing Song 4: Bottom back, feet flat.
I think we've got some bananas to eat. Can you make your hands look like a bunch of bananas? How many bananas have you got? Can you show me?	The children hold their hands up in front, with the fingers facing down, like a bunch of bananas. They wiggle 1 finger at a time, to show how many bananas they have.
We need to put our bananas in a fruit bowl. Can you pretend to make one by putting both hands together like this?	The children turn palms upwards, placing hands side by side in a bowl shape.
Before we eat we are going to make a sign with our hands to say 'Thank you' for the food. Put your hands together and press.	Children place their hands together, matching fingers. They then press 5 times.

NARRATION	ACTIVITY
We're going to make sandwiches for our picnic. First we spread butter on the bread.	The children have a turn at putting some soft spread on a slice of bread.
We're going to cut up some bananas to make them easier to eat. Peel the banana. Now hold it with 1 hand while you cut it with a knife. Watch your fingers!	The children peel and then try chopping bananas on a plate.
Now put the bananas in the bowl. We've got some honey to go with them. Use the twizzle stick to get some out of the jar and put it on your banana in the bowl. Mmm!	The children transfer chopped banana into a bowl, and add some honey, using the twizzle stick. Then they eat bread and honey.

Week 7: What's in the rock pools?

Session A

☀ **Warm-up:** Standing

🦀 **Activity:** Catching the fish

Aims

 To improve pincer grip

 To improve shoulder flexibility and whole arm movements

Equipment needed

 Bubble wrap, ribbon

 Assorted sea creatures, water tray, fishing nets, buckets

NARRATION	WARM-UP
There's lots of seaweed on the beach. Some of it has funny little bubbles that you can squash. Shall we try squashing some of the seaweed with our fingers? Use different fingers to press down – both hands.	Each child has a piece of bubble wrap and has a go at squashing all the bubbles with their fingers. Encourage them to use all fingers, including their little fingers.
Now try squashing the seaweed between your thumb and first finger, on both hands.	The children squash the bubble wrap using a pincer grip.
We could try treading on the seaweed and squashing the bubbles with our toes too.	They try treading on the bubble wrap to squash it with their toes (bare feet will be necessary).
This seaweed is like a big long ribbon. We could use it to draw shapes in the air.	They draw imaginary shapes in the air with their ribbons. You will probably need to give them some ideas.

NARRATION	ACTIVITY
Can you see the little creatures in the water? We are going to try to catch them with our fishing nets and put them in our buckets.	Scooping an assortment of sea creatures out of the water tray using fishing nets and putting into buckets.

Session B

 Warm-up: Sitting

 Activity: Creatures in the sand

Aim

To improve hand and finger strength

Equipment needed

One pair of tongs and bucket per child, sand tray, sea creatures

NARRATION	WARM-UP
Do you remember squashing the seaweed? We squeezed our fingers together. Now we're going to try some more squeezing. Place your hands and fingers together and press, keeping them straight.	The children press hands together as if praying. Press 5 times.
This time curl your fingers over and squeeze your hands together.	Fingers interlocked, squeeze the hands together.
There is a play park over there. Can you see the seesaw? With your fingers still in between each other, can you make them move like a seesaw?	Fingers still interlocked, but this time with fingers on one hand stretched out. Gradually curl those up, and at the same time straighten those on the other hand, giving a seesaw effect.
There are lots of things here that we can squeeze. Let's have a go with them.	The children should try squeezing objects of differing sizes and resistance (e.g. sponge, play dough, different balls).

NARRATION	ACTIVITY
Now we're going to try finding some little creatures in the sand. We'll use something to help us as we don't want to get our fingers nipped. Let's put them into our buckets when we lift them out.	Using a pair of tongs each, the children lift the creatures out of the sand 1 at a time, and put them in their buckets.

Session C

 Warm-up: Sitting

 Activity: Collecting shells

Aims

 To improve finger manipulation

 To improve pincer grip

Equipment needed

 Song 16: Five fishes swam in the ocean so

 Water tray, shells

NARRATION	WARM-UP
There are lots of little fish in the rock pools. Can you see them all swimming about? Let's move our fingers and pretend they are fish.	The children hold up their hands and wiggle their fingers, as if in a swimming action.
Sometimes the fish get hungry, and they like to eat. Then they look like this.	Keeping the heels of the hands together, keep fingers straight and open and close them, like a fish snapping at a piece of food.
Now we are going to sing a song about fishes.	Children sing Song 16: Five fishes swam in the ocean so.

NARRATION	ACTIVITY
I can see some very pretty shells in the rock pools – lots of different colours and sizes. Can you pick them up? Then we will sort them.	The children pick up shells 1 at a time using their fingers, and sort them according to colour, size, shape, etc. They may have more than 1 try at this, using different criteria for sorting each time.

Fine motor week 7

Week 8: Playing games on the beach

Session A

☀ **Warm-up:** Standing

🦀 **Activity:** Completing the fish

Aims

📷 To improve wrist and ankle flexibility

📷 To develop visual perception

Equipment needed

🐚 **Photocopiable 5a** (p. 78) copied on to coloured paper, and **Photocopiable 5b** (p. 79) copied on to a different colour and cut out, Blu-Tack® (1 set per child) – laminating will make this equipment reusable

NARRATION	WARM-UP
We're going to pretend our hands are little fish again. Some of them swim by moving their tails backwards and forwards like this. Can you have a go?	With arms kept fairly still, the children wave their hands backwards and forwards, from side to side, trying to achieve flexibility in their wrists.
I think we could pretend our feet are fish tails as well. Have a go at waving your feet too.	The children now move their feet in all directions, trying to achieve flexibility in their ankles.
Some fish swim like this. See if you can do that too.	Hands together, fingers interlocked. Keeping fingers straight on both hands, waving fingers up and down.

NARRATION	ACTIVITY
We're getting to know all about fish. I think we'll play a fish game now. This fish has got some of its parts missing. Can you find them and fix them on in the right place?	Each child has a copy of Photocopiables 5a and 5b. They select the different parts and press them on to complete the picture.

Fine motor week 8

71

Session B

 Warm-up: Sitting, then standing up

 Activity: Painting a beach ball

Aims

 To develop bilateral co-ordination

 To develop proprioceptive skills

Equipment needed

 Photocopiables 6a and 6b (pp. 80, 81), either on A4 or larger paper, finger paints

NARRATION	WARM-UP
It's good to have a partner to play some games on the beach. Can you find a friend to play with now? Sit down facing each other and stretch out your right hand to meet your partner's right hand. Can you press your hands together? Now change hands and do the same with the other hand.	The children sit facing a partner and stretch a hand across in front diagonally to meet their partner's hand. They press hands together. Then repeat with other hand.
Can you do that again, but this time pat your partner's hand 3 times? Now change hands and do the same on the other side.	Repeat as above, this time patting hands 3 times instead of pressing.
Now we're going to play a game called Bertie Beach Ball Says. You'll have to listen very carefully so that you know what to do.	Play an adaptation of Simon Says, first sitting, then standing up. Try to point to and name lots of different body parts.

NARRATION	ACTIVITY
We're going to paint a big picture of a beach ball using our fingers. Beach balls have lots of different colours in them. Do you know the names of the colours you are painting?	Finger painting, to fill in Photocopiable 6a or 6b. Toe painting may also be attempted.

Fine motor week 8

Session C

 Warm-up: Standing

 Activity: Blow football

Aim

 To develop good breathing control

Equipment needed

 Song 17: Off goes the bubble

Bubble tub and wand per child

Straw per child, A5 piece of scrap paper each to screw into ball, table with central bucket if possible

NARRATION	WARM-UP
Goodness, it's suddenly very windy on the beach! The wind is blowing just like this. I think we know a song about blowing bubbles. Shall we sing it?	The children all have a go at blowing. Then they sing Song 17: Off goes the bubble.
We could try blowing some bubbles. Look how they float away into the sky! Can you catch any of them?	Each child has a bubble wand and blows bubbles, which they then try to catch.
You can make bubbles by waving the wand in the air too. Have a go at that. See whether you can make any patterns in the air.	Wave bubble wand to make different patterns in the air.

NARRATION	ACTIVITY
Now we're going to play a game by blowing through a straw. First you are going to screw up some paper to make a ball. Then, with a partner, you are going to blow the ball to each other across the table.	Each child should have a piece of A5 scrap paper which they screw up into a ball. They then play Blow Football in pairs, using a straw and the paper ball. Both should aim to get the ball backwards and forwards to each other or into the bucket in the middle of the table.

Week 9: Didn't we have a lovely time at the seaside?

Session A

 Warm-up: Sitting at a table

 Activity: Writing in the sand

Aims

 To develop spatial awareness

 To develop basic letter awareness

Equipment needed

Sand tray, small spoon per child, water in jug

NARRATION	WARM-UP
Before we go home we're going to send a postcard to our mums and dads to tell them what a lovely time we've had at the seaside. Perhaps we'd better practise some writing first. Can you draw an 'm' for mum in the air? Try drawing it with the fingers on both hands.	Using their index finger initially, the children copy the shape for 'm' in the air. They then try with different fingers. Then copy different shapes.
Now can you pretend to draw some letters in the sand? Perhaps you could draw the first letter of your name.	The children draw different letter shapes, using different fingers, this time on a horizontal plane – perhaps on the table top.
The sand looks a bit bumpy where we have written our letters. Can you try smoothing it with your hands?	In the air, imaginary smoothing actions with both hands.

NARRATION	ACTIVITY
Now we'll try writing 'm' for mum in the sand. Can you remember what the shape looks like?	Tracing different shapes in the sand, isolating fingers.
Try to write your name in the sand. Can you remember the shape of the letter your name begins with?	Trying to write own name in sand. Try to get each child to trace their initial letter at least and to memorise the shape.
Let's try making some different shapes in the sand using water. Spoon some water out of the jug and make some patterns in the sand.	Using a small spoon, the children get water from a jug and make patterns in the sand.

Session B

 Warm-up: Sitting or standing

 Activity: Sending a postcard

Aims

 To learn simple sequencing skills

 To improve spatial awareness

Equipment needed

 Song 18: Walking on the beach

 Postcards, crayons or finger paints, scissors, **Photocopiable 7** (p. 82), 1 between 2, additional shapes or stickers may be used, 1 stamp roughly cut from **Photocopiable 8** (p. 83) per child, glue

NARRATION	WARM-UP
Let's sing a song about the beach. We can point to all the different things we can see on the beach.	Children sing Song 18: Walking on the beach
Don't forget to tell your mums and dads about the different animals we saw on the beach. We had better remind ourselves about the dog swimming in the sea, the baby seagulls learning to fly and the fish swimming in the rock pools.	The children follow a simple sequence, carrying out the 3 animal actions 1 after the other. Then ask them to repeat.

NARRATION	ACTIVITY
Now it's time to send our postcards home. First we must decorate them to show that they're from the seaside. We mustn't forget to put a stamp on before we post them – the space for the stamp is in the corner.	Children decorate their postcards with pictures from Photocopiable 7 and/or other seaside pictures or stickers and with crayons or finger paints. They cut out the pre-drawn stamp and stick it on the rectangle shape in the corner.

Fine motor week 9

Session C

 Warm-up: Standing

 Activity: Packing the bag

Aim

 To improve proprioceptive skills

Equipment needed

 Song 1: I have two eyes to see with

🐚 **Photocopiable 9** (p. 84) showing small patterned towel, actual small towels, other small items, parachute/blanket, large bag

NARRATION	WARM-UP
It's been such a lovely sunny day that I think we have caught the sun a little – it's a good job we put on some sun cream! We felt the warm sun on different parts of our bodies.	Pointing to different body parts (e.g. nose, elbows, shoulders). Children sing Song 1: I have two eyes to see with.
What has been your favourite part of the seaside adventure? Who would like to show us their favourite part again? We shall watch to see if we can guess what it was.	Children re-enact various activities. If time allows they may want to sing some of their favourite songs.

NARRATION	ACTIVITY
Now that our lovely day has almost come to an end, it's time to collect up and put away our things ready for the journey home. Can you roll up your towel and put it in the bag? Now we need to fold up the blanket so that it will also fit in the bag.	Packing up various items and putting them in the bag, first by rolling and folding paper, then trying with the real item.
Off we go to catch our bus home. We shall make a line at the bus stop. We have had a lovely time at the seaside!	

Fine motor week 9

Session B

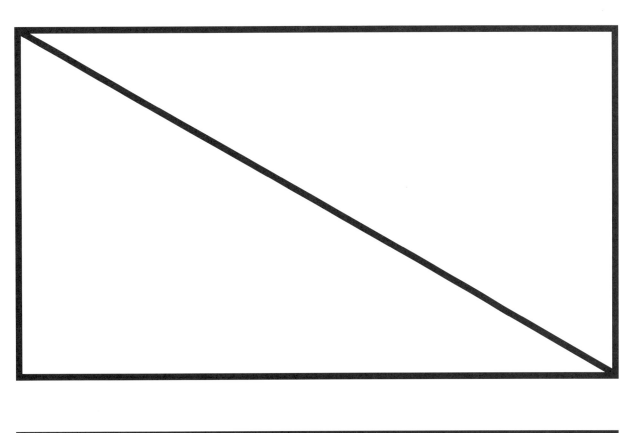

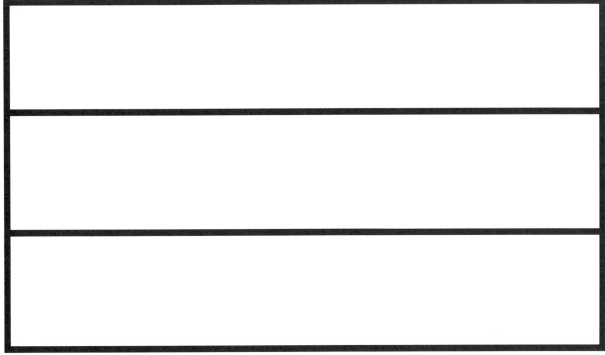

Session A

Session A

Session B

Name .... **Date** ....

Session B

Name .... **Date** ....

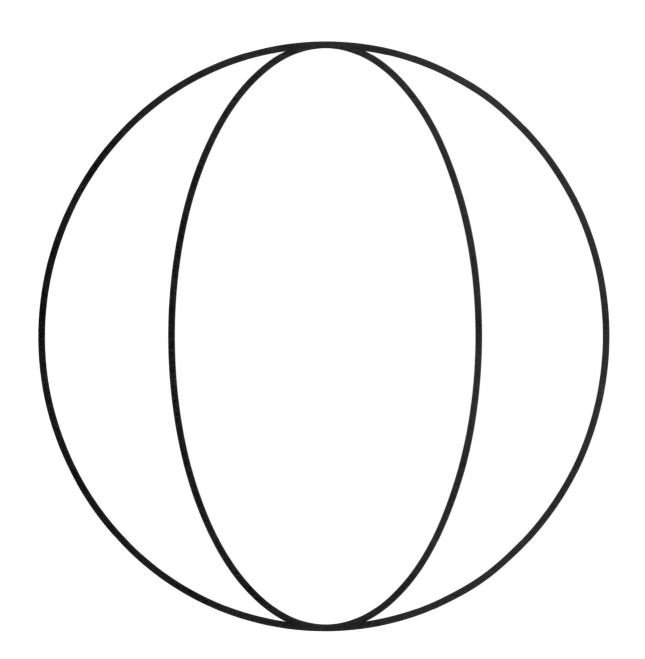

Session B

Session B

Fine Motor Week 9

Session C

Name .... **Date** ....

Songs

Seaside Adventure includes 18 songs, which are an integral part of the programme. All of the songs have appropriate hand and finger actions that have been included specifically to aid the development of motor skills. Many of the melodies are traditional and some are original.

A CD of the songs and music is included with this book. It is organised as follows:

 Tracks 1–18: The songs with both melody and lyrics

Track 19: Seaside medley

Track 20: Seaside atmosphere (relaxing seaside sounds)

Tracks 21–38: Instrumental-only versions of the songs.

This arrangement ensures that the different versions of the songs are easy to find. For example:

Song 1, I have two eyes to see with, is track 1 and track 21 (instrumental),

Song 2, Pat yourself on the back, is track 2 and track 22 (instrumental)

and so on, following this pattern.

The songs on the CD may be used in two ways: for you to sing along with the children or to help you learn the songs, which may then be sung without the CD tracks. The latter suggestion may be useful if you feel that you need to sing the songs more slowly, depending on the capability of your children. The melody line is included in the book as an aid for use if the CD is not played.

'Seaside medley' is a medley of all the songs in an instrumental-only version, to be used when playing the game of Pass the Food Parcel, or at other times if required. This track is much longer than the others and plays for 13 minutes.

'Seaside atmosphere' is a short track (1½ minutes in length) composed especially for the programme. It may be used in the following ways:

 To introduce each session. You could put this music on, and the children will soon recognise it and associate it with the seaside activities.

 As a listening activity to encourage careful listening and identification of sounds heard; for example, seagulls and waves.

 At the end of each gross motor session, when the children are usually asked to lie or sit down quietly and relax.

All songs arranged, performed, recorded and produced by Tim Harding; with Eleanor Harding: vocals, Charlotte Harding: saxophones, keyboards and co-production

• 'Dig, dig, digging in the sand' and 'Wear your sun hat' music and lyrics by Tim Harding
• 'Seaside atmosphere' (instrumental) by Tim Harding
• 'Shake the blanket out' and 'Splishy splashy, splishy splashy' music by Rachel Knight
• 'Wiggle your fingers' music and lyrics by Janet Lee
• 'Five fishes swam in the ocean so' music and lyrics by Lesley Wilkie

Songs

SEASIDE ADVENTURE SONGS AT A GLANCE

Week 1

1 I have two eyes to see with

2 Pat yourself on the back

3 Hello

4 Bottom back, feet flat

5 This is the way we wait for the bus

Week 2

4 Bottom back, feet flat

6 The big red bus

7 The wheels on the bus

Week 3

2 Pat yourself on the back

3 Hello

8 Wear your sun hat

9 This is the way we wash our hands

10 The sun cream song

Week 4

11 Shake the blanket out

12 Wiggle your fingers

13 Splishy splashy, splishy splashy

Week 5

4 Bottom back, feet flat

14 Dig, dig, digging in the sand

Week 6

4 Bottom back, feet flat

15 Two fat seagulls

Week 7

16 Five fishes swam in the ocean so

Week 8

17 Off goes the bubble

Week 9

1 I have two eyes to see with

18 Walking on the beach

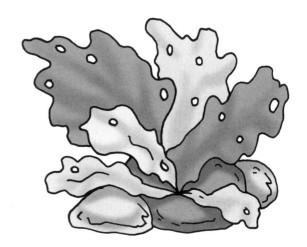

Song 1

I HAVE TWO EYES TO SEE WITH

Use both index fingers to point at eyes, feet, ears and nose

1. **I have two eyes to see with,**
   I have two feet to run.
   I have two ears to hear with,
   A nose – I've only one.

Wave both hands in front as if making a goodbye action.

2. **I have two hands to wave with,**

Use both index fingers to point at mouth, cheeks.

   A mouth to say 'Hello',
   And two red cheeks for you to kiss,

Wave goodbye.

   Then off I go!

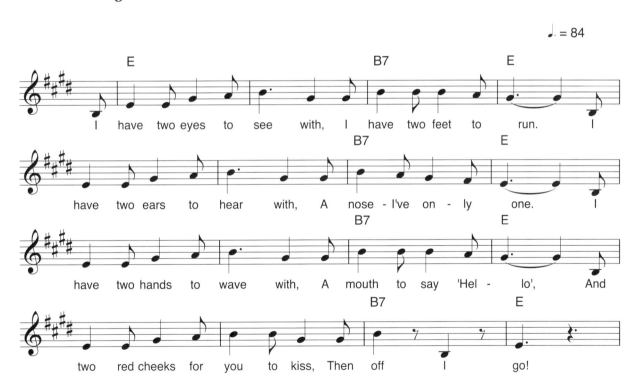

Song 2

PAT YOURSELF ON THE BACK

Pat your back with right hand. Pat your back with left hand.

Pat yourself on the back, on the back.
Pat yourself on the back, on the back.
Pat yourself on the back,

Isolate thumbs on both hands to make 'OK' sign.

Until you get the knack.

Pat your back with both hands.

Pat yourself on the back, on the back.

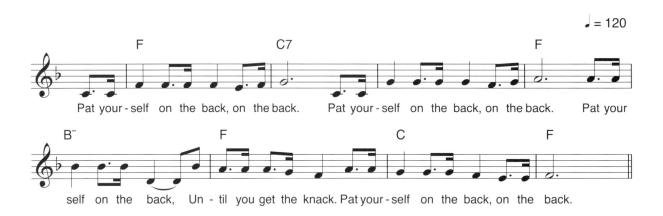

Song 3

HELLO

Hand at shoulder level, sign 'Hello'.

1. **Hello, [child's name]. Hello, [child's name].**

2 hands clasped in front and shake.

   How are you? How are you?

Point at self using index finger.

   Very nice to meet you. Very nice to meet you.

2 hands clasped in front and shake.

   How do you do. How do you do.

Wave goodbye, first 1 hand, then the other.

2. **Goodbye, [child's name]. Goodbye, [child's name].**

Link thumbs together and use fingers to make a flying action.

   Time to fly. Time to fly.

2 hands clasped in front and shake.

   Have a very nice day. Have a very nice day.

Wave goodbye, first 1 hand, then the other.

   Thanks, goodbye. Thanks, goodbye.

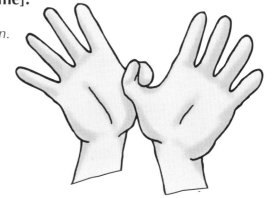

Song 4

BOTTOM BACK, FEET FLAT

Bottom back, feet flat, I am ready.
Bottom back, feet flat, I am ready.
Bottom back, feet flat, I am ready.
Ready to begin.

Song 5

THIS IS THE WAY WE WAIT FOR THE BUS

Stand up and fold arms across chest.

This is the way we wait for the bus,

Put hands on hips.

Wait for the bus, wait for the bus.

Stand up and fold arms across chest.

This is the way we wait for the bus

Put hands on hips.

On a bright and sunny morning.

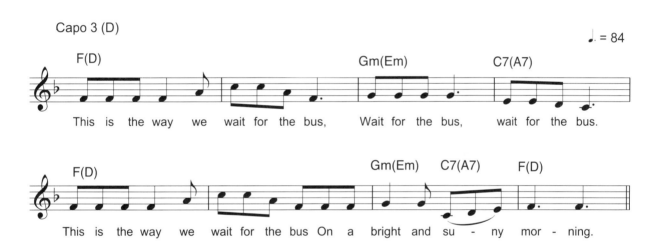

Song 6

THE BIG RED BUS

Arms wide to represent big steering wheel.

1. **Oh, the big red bus goes along a bumpy road,**

Hand draws a wiggly line in front.

Along a bumpy road, along a bumpy road.

Arms wide to represent big steering wheel.

Oh, the big red bus goes along a bumpy road,
Travelling along to the seaside.

Big steering wheel to the left and then to the right.

2. **Oh, the big red bus swerves around a bend,**
   Swerves around a bend, swerves around a bend.
   Oh, the big red bus swerves around a bend,
   Travelling along to the seaside.

Hold up red ball/bead/card in 1 hand for 'Stop'.
Hold up green ball/bead/card in the other hand for 'Start'.

3. **Oh, the big red bus, well it stops and then it starts,**
   It stops and then it starts, it stops and then it starts.
   Oh, the big red bus, well it stops and then it starts,
   Travelling along to the seaside.

Song 7

THE WHEELS ON THE BUS

Hands moving in circular ways (traditional actions).

The wheels on the bus go round and round,
Round and round, round and round.
The wheels on the bus go round and round,
All day long.

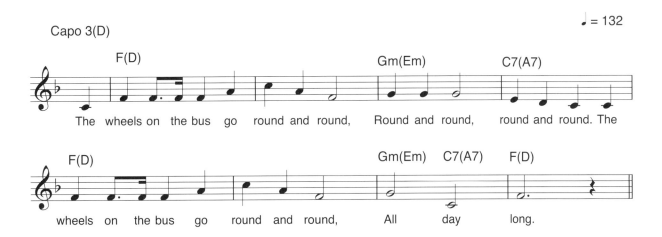

Song 8

WEAR YOUR SUN HAT

Hands in front, move them from left to right and back again as if smoothing the sand.

If you're on the beach, or by the pool,

Stretch both arms up and down towards head as if putting a hat off/on.

Wear your sun hat … and you'll be cool.

Hands in front, move them from left to right and back again as if smoothing the sand.

If you're on the beach, or by the pool,

Stretch both arms up and down towards head as if putting a hat off/on.

Wear your sun hat … and you'll be cool.

Hands wide, shade eyes. With both hands draw a big circle in front to represent the sun.

Its big wide brim will shade your eyes, so when the sun is in the sky

Hands in front, move them from left to right and back again as if smoothing the sand.

And you're on the beach, or by the pool,

Stretch both arms up and down towards head as if putting a hat off/on.

Wear your sun hat … and you'll be cool.

Song 9

THIS IS THE WAY WE WASH OUR HANDS

Rub hands as if washing them.

1. **This is the way we wash our hands,**
   Wash our hands, wash our hands.
   This is the way we wash our hands,
   On a bright and sunny morning.

Shake hands as if drying them.

2. **This is the way we dry our hands,**
   Dry our hands, dry our hands.
   This is the way we dry our hands,
   On a bright and sunny morning.

Song 10

THE SUN CREAM SONG

Use hands to rub parts of the body when named, as if to rub in sun cream.

1. **We rub the sun cream here, the sun cream there,**
   We rub this arm and we rub it everywhere.
   We rub it on our shoulder and our elbow too,
   Rubbing in the sun cream, me and you.

Chorus: Rub, rub, rubbing in the sun cream.
　　　　Rub, rub, rubbing in the sun cream.
　　　　Rub, rub, rubbing in the sun cream.
　　　　Lid off, hand out, squish, squish, squish!

2. **We rub the sun cream here, the sun cream there,**
   We rub our other arm and we rub it everywhere.
   We rub it on our shoulder and our elbow too,
   Rubbing in the sun cream, me and you.

Chorus: Rub, rub, rubbing …

3. **We rub the sun cream here, the sun cream there,**
   We rub this leg and we rub it everywhere.
   We rub it on our knee and on our ankle too,
   Rubbing in the sun cream, me and you.

Chorus: Rub, rub, rubbing …

4. **We rub the sun cream here, the sun cream there,**
   We rub our other leg and we rub it everywhere.
   We rub it on our knee and on our ankle too,
   Rubbing in the sun cream, me and you.

Chorus: Rub, rub, rubbing …

5. **We rub the sun cream here, the sun cream there,**
   We rub our face and we rub it everywhere.
   We rub it on our cheeks and on our noses too,
   Rubbing in the sun cream, me and you.

Chorus: Rub, rub, rubbing …

Song 11

SHAKE THE BLANKET OUT

Using clenched fists as if holding edge of blanket, shake hands in front.

Shake the blanket out, shake the blanket out,
Shake the creases away.
Shake the blanket out, shake the blanket out

Arm outstretched, point to the sky using an index finger.

On this bright, hot sunny day.

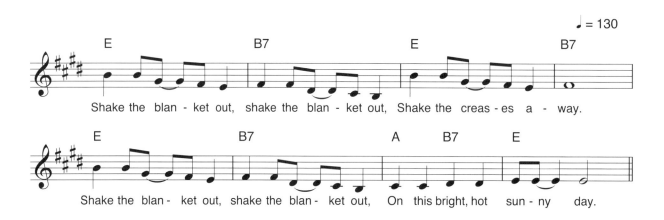

Song 12

WIGGLE YOUR FINGERS

Children wiggle fingers.

Wiggle, wiggle, wiggle, wiggle, wiggle, wiggle, wiggle your fingers.
Wiggle, wiggle, wiggle, wiggle, wiggle, wiggle, wiggle your fingers.
Wiggle your fingers just like me [pause]
Wiggle, wiggle, wiggle, wiggle, wiggle, wiggle, wiggle your fingers.

Song 13

SPLISHY SPLASHY, SPLISHY SPLASHY

Waving hands backwards and forwards, splashing hands in the water.

Splishy splashy, splishy splashy,

Hold 1 hand up to ear to listen.

Can you hear the sea?

Waving hands backwards and forwards, splashing hands in the water.

Splishy splashy, splishy splashy,

Move 1 hand down opposite arm to represent tickling. Repeat with other hand and arm.

Coming to tickle me!

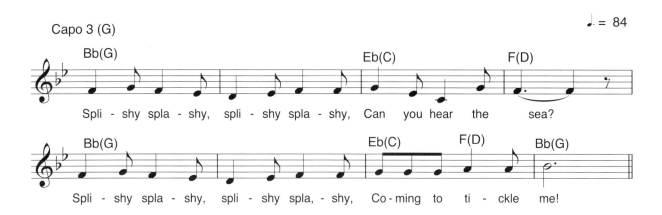

Song 14

DIG, DIG, DIGGING IN THE SAND

Digging action as if with a spade.

Dig, dig, digging in the sand,

Patting action as if patting the sand.

Dig with your spade, pat with your hands.
Building a boat or a castle with a moat,

Digging action as if with a spade.

Dig, dig, digging in the sand.

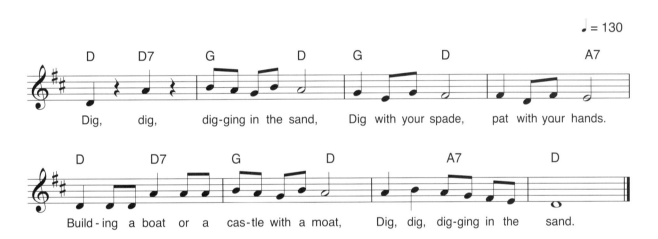

Song 15

TWO FAT SEAGULLS

Curl fingers in front as if to make claws.

1. **Two fat seagulls met on a beach,**

Link thumbs together and flap fingers, nod heads.

Flapped their wings politely and nodded with their beaks.

Make fists using both hands.

Two fat seagulls met on a beach

Link thumbs together and flap fingers.

And flapped their wings politely, two times each.

Curl fingers in front as if to make claws.

2. **Two little seagulls met on a beach,**

Link thumbs together and flap fingers, nod heads.

Flapped their wings politely and nodded with their beaks.

Make fists using both hands.

Two little seagulls met on a beach

Link thumbs together and flap fingers.

And flapped their wings politely, two times each.

Song 16

FIVE FISHES SWAM IN THE OCEAN SO

Use a flat hand to make a horizontal swimming action in front of you.

1. **Five fishes swam in the ocean so,**

Hand 'swims' up and down.

   Up and down, to and fro.

Flapping action with arms at chest level, elbows sticking out as fins, then wriggle with hands together behind back.

   They flapped their fins and wriggled their tails,

Make a large mouth with 1 hand and make it 'eat' 1 finger 'fish'.

   Nobody knew they were frightened of whales.
   How many fish? How many fish?

Make correct number of fish using fingers left.

   How many fish in the sea?

Repeat actions for all verses.

2. **Four fishes swam in the ocean so …**

3. **Three fishes swam in the ocean so …**

4. **Two fishes swam in the ocean so …**

5. **One fish swam in the ocean so,**
   Up and down, to and fro.
   It flapped its fins and wriggled its tail,
   Nobody knew it was frightened of whales.
   No more fish, no more fish, no more fish in the sea.

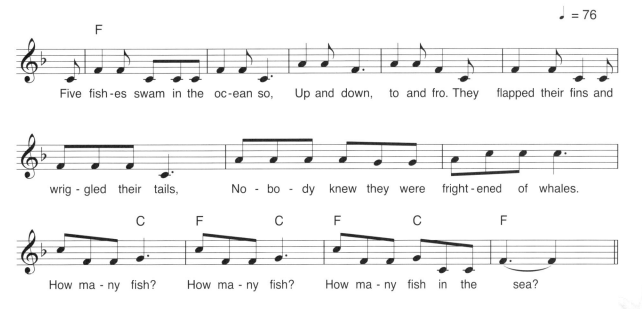

Song 17

OFF GOES THE BUBBLE

Isolate index finger on 1 hand. Make a loose fist shape with other hand and 'dip' in and out.

Get your bubbles ready to blow,
You won't have any trouble.

Lift finger out and pretend to blow a bubble.

Just take a breath [breathe in]
And blow it out [blow out] –

Draw a spiral shape in the air with index finger.

Off goes the bubble!

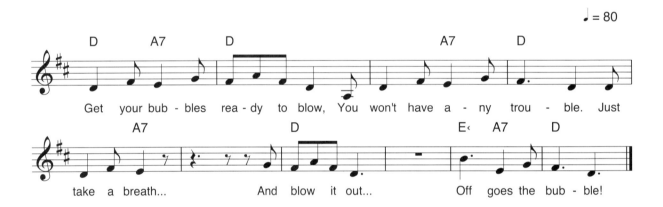

Song 18

WALKING ON THE BEACH

Marching on the spot.
Walking on the beach, walking on the beach,

Hand to head as if looking.
Look, look, what did we see?

Marching on the spot.
Walking on the beach, walking on the beach,

Hand to head as if looking.
Look, look, what did we see?

Point to the air, then to floor, with outstretched arm and index finger.
Point to the seagull, point to the sand,

Point to the distance, then wave.
Point to the blue sea, wave your hand.

Clap hands together, pat knees using both hands.
Clap your hands, pat your knees,

2 hands outstretched, palms up as if asking.
Can we come back another day, please?

Repeat actions as beginning.
Walking on the beach, walking on the beach,
Look, look, what did we see?
Walking on the beach, walking on the beach,
Look, look, what did we see?

4 Additional guidance

Dressing skills

As a result of screening you will have noted those children who have the greatest difficulty with dressing and undressing. If at all possible, try to develop the skills of these children, perhaps when they are changing for PE. Children with a diagnosed physical difficulty may require a certain way of dressing, and you should therefore liaise with their therapists.

You may wish to work through the list of skills on the dressing skills record sheet (**Photocopiable 10**, p. 108). Use it to record the progress of children whom you have identified as having difficulties by ticking the box when they have demonstrated a particular skill. The dressing skills target sheet (**Photocopiable 11**, p. 109) may be used to write down targets for children as they progress through the dressing skills.

Another way in which you can help children is by using a method known as backward chaining. The child learns the final part of the particular skill first, and then gradually increases their ability by doing a little more each time until eventually they are able to complete the whole task independently.

Here is an example of learning to put on a sock using backward chaining:

1   Put sock on child's foot over toes and heel. Encourage child to pull up sock from ankle.

2   Put sock on, just covering the toe and instep but not the heel. The child pulls the sock up from here.

3   The sock is put on just covering the toes. The child pulls the sock up from here.

4   The sock is given to the child, gathered up so their toes go straight into the bottom. The child takes the gathered sock and puts it on themselves.

5   The child puts on the sock totally independently.

Dressing skills record sheet

DRESSING SKILL	Name									
Removes socks										
Tries to put on shoe										
Finds armhole										
Removes unfastened shirt										
Helps push trousers down										
Purposely removes shoe if fastenings undone										
Puts on coat/cardigan/sweater (not fastenings)										
Removes elastic-waisted pants or trousers										
Tries to put on socks										
Unfastens large button										
Finds front of clothing										
Puts on T-shirt										
Pulls down trousers/pants to remove them										
Puts on socks, but difficulty with heel										
Puts on shoes, but cannot do fastenings										
Fastens large button										
Puts on pants or trousers independently, but not right way round										
Removes jumper										
Knows front and back consistently										
Turns clothing right side out										
Puts on socks with no assistance										

 Permission to Photocopy

11

Dressing skills target sheet

CHILD'S NAME	TARGET

Developing ball skills

Ball skills are generic activities of:

- ✦ spatial awareness (moving safely and effectively in the playing area);
- ✦ sending (rolling, throwing, striking/hitting or kicking);
- ✦ receiving (catching, stopping and controlling or trapping).

The equipment used for these activities may be beanbags, fluff balls, scarves, tail balls, koosh balls, airflow balls, tennis balls, bump balls, sensory balls, sponge balls or any ball appropriate to the activity and ability of the child.

Suggestions for developing ball skills are given in the following chart.

Ball skills chart

SENSORY EXPERIENCES	SPATIAL AWARENESS ACTIVITIES
1. Roll ball over foot, up leg, around waist, down other leg, over foot, up back of leg, down back of leg; roll around neck, around waist, around one leg, around the other leg. **2.** Move in and out of other pupils, carrying beanbag on different parts of body. **3.** Call out colours of beanbags to collect and place on shoulder.	**1.** Children move in and out of spots on the floor without touching them; on a signal they stop on a spot. **2.** Move in and out of spots carrying a ball; on a signal put the ball on a spot so it is still; repeat, going back to the same spot or to a new spot each time. (Make this activity easier by using beanbags instead of balls; vary the activity by propelling the ball with the hand along the floor – 'take ball for a walk'). **3.** Place a variety of small games equipment around the space. On command children collect the item named (e.g. red beanbag) and put it into a designated box, area or hoop; movement could be limited by allowing walking only. **4.** Keep the box full: soft items (e.g. koosh balls, small beanbags) are thrown carefully one at a time by the practitioner; the children collect one at a time and return them to the box; the children win if they always have something in the box (check safety carefully as children are moving in a confined space).

ACQUIRING AND DEVELOPING SKILLS	APPLICATION OF SKILLS	TEACHING POINTS

ROLLING

1. Children roll ball into a space, chase and pick up; emphasise need not to roll ball too far (check all rolling is the same direction and not crossing paths). **2.** Roll ball into a space, run past ball, turn and gather/collect ball with two hands, then carry ball back to place. **3.** Children roll ball under 'bridges' (made with two cones and a cane), then try to get round bridge to collect ball. **4.** In pairs with two parallel benches, roll large ball along gap between the benches and catch at the end. **5.** To make this more difficult, both children begin at the same end of the bench; one rolls and the other runs to catch it at the opposite end.	**1.** In pairs roll ball for partner into space, partner runs past it, stops ball, controls it and returns it to partner. Repeat 3–4 times, then change over. **2.** In a small circle a child calls name of receiver, rolls ball across circle, following through with hands after ball; receiver crouches and stops ball using two hands.	**Roll** **1.** Opposite foot to throwing hand forward. **2.** Crouch low. **3.** Swing arm from back to front. **4.** Point hand in direction of roll to follow through. **Collect or gather** **1.** Move in front of the rolling ball. **2.** Crouch down with feet together. **3.** With two hands together, make a round basket. **4.** Grasp the ball in fingers.

THROWING UNDERARM

1. In pairs underarm toss over bridge, without knocking cane down; use fluff ball or beanbag squashed into hand and held like a ball. **2.** Throw a beanbag underarm to land on a spot on the ground; move back a step and repeat (try to get beanbag 'dropping' onto spot rather than sliding across floor). **3.** In pairs one child rolls ball under bridge, follows, stops and gathers up, throws over bridge, partner collects and repeats. **4.** In pairs with a larger ball, send ball 'low to high' away from body (in a rainbow shape) using two hands. 5. In pairs throw underarm to partner, allowing ball to bounce before catching.	**1.** In a small group, throw underarm to practitioner in centre of circle. **2.** In a short line, starting from the back, pass or throw a ball or beanbag underarm to child in front; when it gets to the front of the line the child runs to the back of line and starts again (use mat spots to space children and give them a location). **3.** Pass a ball along line sideways, and at the end run to the opposite end and start again; widen gaps, develop underarm throw work to left and right.	**1.** Curl thumb and fingers around ball or beanbag. **2.** Start with hand back, opposite foot to throwing hand. **3.** Swing low to high and away in a rainbow shape. **4.** Point arm where ball needs to go, to partner or target. **Two-handed underarm throw** **1.** As above, but movement starts at side of body, with two hands. **2.** 'Give' at knees. **Catch** **1.** With two hands together and little fingers touching, make a basket. **2.** Watch pathway of ball. **3.** Move hands to meet ball and 'give' to cushion ball. **4.** For a larger ball hands need to be further apart.

ACQUIRING AND DEVELOPING SKILLS	APPLICATION OF SKILLS	TEACHING POINTS

BOUNCE AND CATCH

1. Using one large ball each sit on the ground and bounce between legs and catch, then repeat while high kneeling, then standing. **2.** Toss ball up underarm, let ball bounce, then catch. **3.** Toss ball up, let it bounce, clap hands and catch. **4.** Bounce ball in hoop and catch, then repeat while walking around the hoop. **5.** Pat bouncing using one ball each. **6.** If a wall is available, throw the ball up against it, allow it to bounce and catch. **7.** In a small circle, bounce ball across for another child to catch.	**1.** In a small group, underarm pass from practitioner in centre of circle, receiver bounces pass back. **2.** Repeat and run or walk around outside of circle back to place. **3.** Pass from centre of circle and return using same pass: bounce, underarm or roll. **4.** Toss beanbag, scarf, tail ball, small or large ball up, catch with two hands. **5.** Different activity per mat, children in pairs: • roll under 'bridge'; • play throw and catch; • toss beanbag through or into hoop; • roll and knock down skittles.	**Two-handed push or bounce pass** **1.** Two hands on ball. **2.** Step forwards and push ball down and away. **3.** Extend arms in direction of target (e.g. partner). **Bounce to self** **1.** Two hands on ball. **2.** Push ball down close to feet. **3.** Extend arms downward; ball to bounce to waist height.

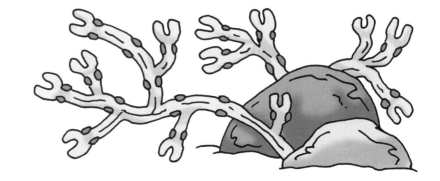

Guidelines for gross motor development

Age between 2 and 3 years

It should be understood that 2-year-old children will vary enormously in their development of motor skills. There is a huge difference between what some children are able to do at the age of 2 and at 2½ years.

Between 2 and 2½ years:

- ✿ able to walk backwards
- ✿ learning to run
- ✿ walk upstairs and downstairs holding on to rail or wall, one step at a time (i.e. both feet on to each step)
- ✿ squat with complete steadiness to rest or to play with objects and rise to feet without using hands
- ✿ able to stand on a low beam
- ✿ climb up on to furniture
- ✿ can push and pull large wheeled toys; can pull small wheeled toy by cord
- ✿ throw small ball overhand and forwards, without falling over
- ✿ walk into a large ball when attempting to kick it
- ✿ explore new movement patterns.

Between 2½ and 3 years:

- ✿ run on whole foot, stopping and starting with ease and avoiding obstacles
- ✿ walk upstairs confidently and downstairs holding on to rail, one step at a time (i.e. both feet on to each step)
- ✿ can stand on tiptoes if shown how
- ✿ can jump from a low step/surface with both feet together
- ✿ climb easy nursery equipment
- ✿ sit on small tricycle and steer, using feet to push along
- ✿ throw ball from hand somewhat stiffly at body level
- ✿ kick a ball gently, without falling over
- ✿ begin to integrate entire body on activities concentrating on complex movements.

Age 3 years

Able to:

- ✪ walk backwards, forwards and sideways, arms alongside the body
- ✪ walk along a line for 3 m
- ✪ stand or walk on balls of feet, heels raised, with arms moving loosely at sides
- ✪ run a distance of 10 m without falling over
- ✪ balance on either foot momentarily
- ✪ jump on the spot and from a low step, keeping the feet together
- ✪ climb up stairs / climbing frame in an adult fashion, placing one foot on each step consecutively
- ✪ come down stairs one step at a time (i.e. both feet on to each step)
- ✪ pedal a tricycle and change direction appropriately
- ✪ throw a ball
- ✪ catch a large ball on or between extended hands
- ✪ kick a ball forcibly
- ✪ carry out 3 tasks when shown and instructed (e.g. clap hands 3 times, take 3 steps and turn around)
- ✪ sit with legs out straight in front, pick up a beanbag from one side of the body and place it (not throw) on the floor on the other side of the body.

Age 4 years

Able to:

- ✪ stand, walk or run on balls of feet, heels raised, with arms moving loosely at sides
- ✪ walk along a line for at least 8 steps, on balls of feet, heels raised
- ✪ run a distance of at least 10 m without falling over
- ✪ balance on one leg (usually dominant leg) for 3–5 seconds
- ✪ jump over a cane at knee height (approx. 25 cm high), taking off with feet together and landing with or without feet together
- ✪ walk up and down stairs in an adult fashion, placing one foot on each step consecutively, initially holding the rail
- ✪ ride a tricycle expertly, including making U turns
- ✪ show increasing skill with a ball and use a bat
- ✪ catch a beanbag either cleanly in hands or gathered to the chest
- ✪ show constant improvement in kicking skills
- ✪ carry out 3 tasks when shown and instructed (e.g. clap hands 3 times, take 3 steps and turn around) – from age 3
- ✪ sit with legs out straight in front, pick up a beanbag from one side of the body and place it (not throw) on the floor on the other side of the body – from age 3.

Age 5 years

Able to:

- balance on one leg for 8–10 seconds
- run lightly on balls of feet, heels raised
- walk along a line for at least 9 steps, on balls of feet, heels raised
- walk sideways by crossing one foot over the other
- hop on either foot for 2–3 metres
- skip
- jump over a cane at knee height (approx. 25 cm high), taking off and landing with feet together
- move from half-kneeling (on one knee, opposite foot forward and flat on floor) to standing, without using hands
- walk up and down stairs in an adult fashion, placing one foot on each step consecutively
- play ball games with rules
- catch a beanbag cleanly (i.e. in hands and not clasped to the chest)
- stop and trap a large ball using one foot
- carry out three tasks when shown and instructed (e.g. clap hands 3 times, take 3 steps and turn around) – from age 3
- attempt to dance rhythmically to music.

Guidelines for fine motor development

Age between 2 and 3 years

It should be understood that 2-year-old children will vary enormously in their development of motor skills. There is a huge difference between what some children are able to do at the age of 2 years and at 2½ years.

Between 2 and 2½ years

Manipulative skills

- ❂ Builds a tower of about six blocks.
- ❂ Picks up tiny objects and quickly puts them down.
- ❂ Completes a 6-piece inset puzzle.

Pencil skills

- ❂ Holds pencil well down the shaft using thumb and first two fingers (primitive tripod grasp).
- ❂ Makes spontaneous circular scribble, to and fro scribble and dots.
- ❂ Able to imitate a vertical line.

Self-care

- ❂ Feeds self competently with a spoon. Lifts open cup and drinks well without spilling.
- ❂ Indicates need to go to the toilet.

Between 2½ and 3 years

Manipulative skills

- ❂ Builds a tower of six to eight blocks.
- ❂ Picks up tiny objects accurately, using a fine pincer grasp, and quickly puts them down with increasing skill.
- ❂ Begins to fit together two interlocking pieces of puzzle.
- ❂ Threads large beads on to thick lace.

Pencil skills

- ❂ Holds pencil in preferred hand with improved tripod grasp.
- ❂ Increasing pencil control.
- ❂ Able to imitate a horizontal line.
- ❂ Roughly copies a circle.

Self-care

- ❂ Eats skilfully with a spoon and may use a fork.
- ❂ Uses potty or toilet consistently to soil. Pulls down pants for using the toilet.

Age 3 years

Able to:

- ☢ build a tower of 9 x 2.5 cm bricks
- ☢ copy bridge with bricks
- ☢ close fist and wiggle thumb
- ☢ unscrew 2.5 cm diameter lid/barrel
- ☢ thread large bead on to lace
- ☢ snip with scissors.

Pencil skills

Able to:

- ☢ achieve static tripod grasp
- ☢ imitate a circle
- ☢ draw a person with one or two features.

Self-care

Able to:

- ☢ eat with fork and spoon
- ☢ find arm and leg holes in clothes
- ☢ put on T-shirt and socks
- ☢ partly achieve with supervision going to toilet, brushing teeth and hair.

Age 4 years

Able to:

- ✿ show hand preference, usually consistently, sometimes fully established
- ✿ build a tower of 10 x 2.5 cm bricks
- ✿ copy bridge – from age 3
- ✿ unscrew 2.5 cm diameter lid/barrel – from age 3
- ✿ lace sewing cards
- ✿ thread small beads on to lace
- ✿ place small pellets into bottle
- ✿ achieve finger to thumb opposition – imitates spreading of hand and bringing thumb to each finger in turn
- ✿ transfer an object from palm to fingers and fingers to palm
- ✿ cut along a line
- ✿ cut out a triangle/square
- ✿ use tweezers/hammers
- ✿ complete 6–9 piece form board
- ✿ complete 12-piece jigsaw
- ✿ name various colours.

Pencil skills

Able to:

- ✿ achieve tripod grip on pencil
- ✿ copy □ ○ +
- ✿ draw a person with head, legs, trunk and sometimes arms and fingers
- ✿ show some pencil control – can contain pencil within narrow track
- ✿ connect dot to dot, drawing a straight line.

Self-care

Able to:

- ✿ use spoon skilfully
- ✿ begin to use knife and fork
- ✿ dress and undress with a little help
- ✿ know front and back
- ✿ buckle shoes/belt
- ✿ undo and fasten large buttons in full view (on front), but still needs help with tying laces, ties, small buttons and back buttons
- ✿ use the toilet independently
- ✿ wash and dry hands and face
- ✿ comb hair
- ✿ brush teeth.

Age 5 years

Able to:

- ☼ maintain hand preference consistently
- ☼ build tower of 10 x 2.5 cm bricks – from age 4
- ☼ copy steps and pyramid with cubes/bricks
- ☼ use ruler and pencil sharpener
- ☼ fold paper in half lengthways
- ☼ count the fingers on one hand with the index finger of the other
- ☼ thread small beads on to fine lace
- ☼ thread large needle
- ☼ know left and right
- ☼ cut along curved line
- ☼ cut out 5 cm diameter circle
- ☼ cut out simple picture.

Pencil skills

Able to:

- ☼ colour between vertical lines
- ☼ use dynamic tripod grip, usually consistently
- ☼ draw a house with door, windows and chimney
- ☼ copy □ ○ △
- ☼ write a few letters from memory
- ☼ copy simple words
- ☼ copy V, T, H, O, X, L, A, C, U, Y
- ☼ draw a man with head, trunk, legs, arms and fingers, feet and features.

Self-care

Able to:

- ☼ use knife and fork skilfully
- ☼ tie simple overhand knot
- ☼ tie laces (possibly)
- ☼ put zipper teeth into fastener
- ☼ button and unbutton own clothing (buttons in front)
- ☼ use knife to spread butter on toast.

Glossary of terms

Auditory perception – ability to process information received through hearing.

Bilateral – involvement of both sides of the body.

Co-ordination – muscles working together to achieve smooth, efficient movements.

Developmental co-ordination disorder (DCD) – impairment, immaturity or disorganisation of movement, which leads to difficulties in co-ordination. It may affect both fine and gross motor competencies and there may be other associated problems.

Dominance – relates to the side of the body that a child favours to carry out activities requiring one side (e.g. handwriting, using a spoon, kicking a ball).

Dyspraxia – poor ability to motor plan, with many associated difficulties.

Extension – stretching of the muscles to achieve straightening out of back, arm, leg, etc.

Fine motor skills – small, often intricate, movement of the hands and fingers.

Flexion – tightening of muscles to achieve bending or pulling in of parts of the body.

Gross motor skills – large movements of the body and limbs (e.g. running, hopping, catching a ball).

Midline – invisible line down the centre of the body separating the body into right and left sides

Midline crossing – ability to cross hand from one side of the body to the other, required in activities such as handwriting.

Perception – ability of the brain to interpret sensory input.

Prone – lying with the body face down.

Proprioception – ability of the brain to interpret messages from muscles and joints, enabling awareness of where each part of the body is and how it is moving.

Proximal stability – strength and stability of the core, trunk and back muscles of the body (those close to the centre of the body).

Reciprocal movement – two-sided action where the movements of one side of the body complement those of the opposite side.

Supine – lying with the body face up.

Trunk stability – see *proximal stability*.

Visual perception – ability to process information received through vision.

References

Burrows, H., S. Christie, S. Orr and Y. Ostermeyer (2009) *The Jungle Journey*, LDA

Goddard Blythe, S. (2000) 'Early Learning in the Balance: Priming the First ABC', *Support for Learning* 15 (4)

Goddard Blythe, S. (2004) *The Well Balanced Child*, Hawthorn Press

Macintyre, C. and K. McVitty (2004) *Movement and Learning in the Early Years*, Paul Chapman

Nicolson, R. and A. Fawcett (2004) *The Dyslexia Early Screening Test*, Harcourt

Palmer, S. (2006) *Toxic Childhood*, Orion Books

Portwood, M. (2004) 'Movement Disorders in Early Childhood – an Epidemic', *The Dyspraxia Foundation Professional Journal* 3

Sheridan, M.D. (1992) *From Birth to Five Years*, Routledge

Further reading

Addy, L. (2003) *How to Understand and Support Children with Dyspraxia*, LDA

Ball, M. (2004) *Developmental Coordination Disorder*, Jessica Kingsley

Chambers, M. and D. Sugden (2006) *Early Years Movement Skills*, Whurr

Dixon, G. and L. Addy (2004) *Making Inclusion Work for Children with Dyspraxia*, RoutledgeFalmer

Drew, S. (2005) *Including Children with Developmental Coordination Disorder (Dyspraxia) in the Foundation Stage*, Featherstone Education Ltd

Jones, N. (ed.) (2005) *Developing School Provision for Children with Dyspraxia – a Practical Guide*, Paul Chapman

Kirby, A. (1999) *Dyspraxia – the Hidden Handicap*, Souvenir Press (E&A) Ltd

Kirby, A. and S. Drew (2003) *Guide to Dyspraxia and Developmental Coordination Disorders*, David Fulton

Lee, M. (2004) *Coordination Difficulties – Practical Ways Forward*, David Fulton

Macintyre, C. (2000) *Dyspraxia in the Early Years*, David Fulton

Portwood, M. (1999) *Developmental Dyspraxia Identification and Intervention*, 2nd edn, David Fulton

Portwood, M. (2000) *Understanding Developmental Dyspraxia – a Textbook for Students and Professionals*, David Fulton

Ripley, K. (2001) *Inclusion for Children with Dyspraxia/DCD – a Handbook for Teachers*, David Fulton

Sheridan, M.D. (1999) *Play in Early Childhood*, Routledge